Contents

PART 1

The Last American (Married) Pope 1
Afterward at the Motel 6
My Friend 9
The Working Honeymoon 11
In the Living Room 14
Joe's First Wife 15
Together Again 19
Native American Employment 22
Late Afternoon Office Check In 24
Deacon Joe at the Home of Pedro Hernandez 26
Joe Quotes 29
Appearance of the Holy Spirit 30
Joe's Letter to Milly 31
Author's Notes 32
Pope Joseph Speaks to Crowd 35

PART 2

The New Pope Continues 40
The Next Sunday's Sermon 43
Newspaper and TV Interview 45
My First Letter to the Bishops of Our Catholic Church 50
The Pope at the Pentecost Mass 51

Conception 53
Woman? 56
Stroll Through the Vatican Garden 58
Next Day: Milly in Bed. 61
Thinking. 63
Sermon: Mass of Corpus Christi (World TV) 64
Notes of Mike Wyschochek, the Author 66
Hell 69
On the Throne. 70
A Letter to the Bishops of Our Catholic Church. 72
Love 74
The Bishop's Inquiry 77
Praise 79
The Last Words of David 80
A Few Days Later 81
Letter to Members of the Catholic Congress 82
Questions: Why Has the Holy Ghost Hidden From Us? 83
Correction 86
Small Meeting with Newspapermen 87
At a Later Sunday Sermon at the Vatican 90
Walking in a Large Courtyard, Guards Twenty Feet Behind 93
The Records Via Mike. 95
To Pray (Sunday Sermon). 96
At a Private Meeting with the Pope
(Omitting Spanish and Translations) 98
Interview Continued the Next Week 100
To the Bishops of Our Catholic Church 104
Mike Wyschochek—The Author 105
Broke 107

The Last American Pope

The Last American Pope

MIKE WYSCHOCHEK

PALMETTO
PUBLISHING
Charleston, SC
www.PalmettoPublishing.com

© 2024 by Mike Wyschochek

All rights reserved. This book or any portion thereof may not be reproduced or used in any manner whatsoever without the express written permission of the publisher except for the use of brief quotations in a book review.

Hardcover ISBN: 979-8-8229-2969-2
Paperback ISBN: 979-8-8229-2970-8
eBook ISBN: 979-8-8229-2971-5

Summary of the Last American (Married) Pope

I have been the friend of Pope Joseph for nearly fifty years. I met Joe as a poor brokenhearted kid just out of college. We worked together on the reservation. Then he was off to the army. He got married and had four kids. His businesses over the years made him millions. We worked together here and there until his wife died. Then we teamed up for his great crusade: to help Native Americans. He put his heart and soul into our nonprofit business, but it really took off when his college sweetheart joined us. Milly took over the inside part of the business. Joe did the public relations and management. I did the miles of legwork and investigations. Millions of dollars came in from everywhere. Joe became a newsmaker. Then there was their incredible wedding—so much love, so much fun. Their great love of God, of each other, and of all of us led the Holy Spirit into choosing Joe to be the last pope.

I asked Joe, "Are you a women's libber? Your wife is running the Vatican, a longtime male holdout. You have given women authority all over the church, even making women priests. Most of all, you have exposed the Holy Spirit as a woman, our Mother, that longtime Vatican secret."

Joe said, "You know me; I treat everyone equally, even children."

"Is that because you are American or because you're Christian?"

"Both."

"And being the pope is a dangerous job?"

"The Holy Spirit is with me."

And so she must be, as he rushes about the world, preparing people for the end of time, teaching about the simplicity of living and the great love of the Holy Spirit, the incredible Mother of all love. "Love is God's password."

Joe and Milly are attacked from all sides. Should a pope tell people to stop having babies for awhile? But Joe struggles on anyway. It is his new crusade. Joe and Milly are wounded, they suffer, but they survive. They prepare themselves, "We want to meet Christ; he is coming. We must warn the world."

Joe thinks deeply. He loves deeply, but he is also practical. He is sitting at the edge of the end of our civilization. Yet he knows the answer. He has stood up against the drug lords and the Mafia. He has gone against tradition and, because of God's revelation, has defied normal logic, yet stands up as the super salesman he is, as the army officer he was, and as the last pope he is.

With a wife of such incredible qualities as one bishop says, "If we could know a pope's wife could be this virtuous and competent, we should recommend all popes have a wife."

I love them both so much; I love Milly's housekeeper even more. Yet we can never be together again. The world is coming apart. I must continue to serve in my soup kitchen. Somebody must be alive to see Christ's coming.

Joe and Milly will be there, the last pope, and his wife and lovers, together again.

Author's Note

As logical and beautiful as this author makes it seem, the Christian church has not discussed the identity of the Holy Spirit. Being a story of the near future, it is only part fiction in the author's mind and heart. My quote: "Is there a complete, fulfilled, loving family without a mother?" Catholic sermon quote: "God is a family." Creed quote: "The giver of all life." Definition of a mother.

Joe and Milly in Their Bedroom Embracing 109
News 111
The Call to Arms 113
A Few Rare Moments Alone Together in the Garden. 115
Letter from the Betrayer to Pope Joseph. 117
Alone Before the Evening Meal 118
The End Times 120
Last Letter from Mike. 126
The Beginning of the End. 127
My Letter 129

Part 1

The Last American (Married) Pope

I was there at the St. Pius X chapel in Flagstaff for the marriage of Grandpa Joe and Grandma Milly, apart for forty years. My friend Joe and all his children and grandchildren on one side of the church; wonderful jolly Milly and her children and grandchildren were on the other side of the church. Hundreds of friends, coworkers, family, and a delegation of Navajos and other VIPs were there. Joe and Milly were to be important people. Their love and dedication were winning.

Down the west aisle walked Milly, surrounded by her five children. They were greeted by childish giggles and laughter, then applause.

Joe walked down the north aisle with his four children. Then his noisy grandchildren rushed up to the alter behind them and sat down. Then the other grandchildren rushed up too.

That country guitar music started, and the whiny voice cried out the song, "Together-again." We stood there with tears in our eyes, almost crying.

Joe and Milly stood there holding hands in the spotlight, smiling to us, waving at us, calling out names.

We cheered, and we clapped. It was like the big game, and our side won.

After the mass, the ceremony, and the priest's talk, Joe picked up a baby and said, "This is our newest grandchild...by Milly's daughter Judy. He is special; he will be my first baptism when I become a deacon in three weeks. You are all invited to another get-together."

Wait.

"Forty years ago, this wonderful woman and I were deeply in love," said Joe. "We were both students, very poor. Our engagement ring was that glass ring you can see around her neck. I somehow saved it all these years.

"But it was my fault we broke up. I sinned greatly. I offended God.

"Some of you don't know what it is to walk through life hand-in-hand with God, to always be there, to answer questions. When we asked for money to help the Navajos, we got millions of dollars. When we asked for a way to help, it was shown to us. God is my closest friend.

"I had been bouncing through life with no goal. But I have been learning. I found another woman I could care about. Many of you know her caring and understanding. God said Anna is now living within happiness and love.

"But I, in my romantic youth, my silliness, my immaturity—I loved this woman...too much.

"Christ said, "Love God with your whole heart, your whole mind, your whole being. I loved this woman with my whole heart, my whole mind, my whole being. I offended God...my best friend.

"God, my parent, my friend, had to straighten me out. He changed her mind, he made her see me as a poor, silly, childish fool... too possessive...not a good parent for her children. She moved away.

"I was broken. God had to save me. I mentally withdrew inside my pain. God had to save me.

"So I took the job far away, down here on the Navajo Reservation. These people befriended me. They gave me—a stranger, a white man—support and comfort, maybe even a daughter, but nothing ever worked out.

"I asked God to someday repay them. He has given me the chance. Many of you work with us in our company, The Fund for the Employment of Native Americans. We help native businessmen. We train people for jobs. We have started factories to employ Navajos. We will start a nursing school. Milly is at my side.

"Remember the forty years of Moses in the desert to straighten out his people? God gave me forty years to straighten myself out. My love has been spread out in many directions, to many people. Thus, he allowed Milly and me back together again.

"Christ had two points to his saying. 'Love God with your whole heart and soul, love thy neighbors as yourself.' God has shown me the way to do both. God will help us with our great crusade.

"God be with us all."

After a long quiet space, Milly stood up to speak.

"God gave me a husband who worked hard and kept us on the right path. God said he isn't living in happiness yet, but he will be. He needs our prayers. Larry told me to remarry—for love. Those of you who resent this marriage should know I love this man too.

"God talks to Joe and me. We are friends. You can bring this happiness to yourself too. But you must take that great step into empty space, to love the unknown, to ask God to love this unknown more, to love oneself less, to love things less. That is a very hard thing to do. To put your trust in what you cannot see.

"You see Joe's big house and cars and all his things, and you ask, 'Wait a minute?' But those things are for the business to impress customers and donators. We will be selling all this excess baggage and moving to an apartment. We need money to employ the poor, to give them self-worth.

"And if we die without any money, you should cheer at our success. You should cheer that we are together again…Joe, myself, and God.

"Go into your deepest heart and ask God: 'My God, help me love you more…more…more…more. Then you will find him."

As Milly sat down, again came that whiny song, "Together Again," we were in tears again.

Then all stood up for a few pictures, and off to the Little America Ballroom and the feast, drinking and toasting the giant sign "Together Again."

Joe stood up to thank us and to tell a story. "When I first came down to the reservation, I met my friend Mike (pointing to me). We went around to a lot of places. Then he said, "Let's go to a Navajo wedding. He knew the groom, a teacher, as a drinking friend. It was to be a shotgun wedding. So we drove way out in the country—winding dirt roads for miles—and came to an old stone chapter house. Many people still had horses and wagons. There was the strong smell of greasy mutton stew as we walked in.

"On a blanket on the floor sat the bride, as beautiful as you can imagine a human being could be. When everyone was settled, a rickety, bowlegged old man came in, nicely dressed in lots of jewelry. He was the medicine man; he blessed the blanket area and the woman, waving feathers and chanting.

"Then from outside came the groom. A Navajo marine was at each arm, almost carrying him in. They helped him sit down on the blanket. The medicine man sat and blessed them with yellow dust and spoke to the woman, and she agreed.

"Then, in guttural broken English, he asked 'So you take this woman to be your wife?'

The crowd roared at this weird accent. 'Don't want to marry no woman.'

"The crowd laughed themselves to tears.

"The two marines twisted his ears and said, 'Shut up.'

"The medicine man shook his feathers and talked in Navajo and said to the man, 'This is your wife.'

"'No.'

"'Yes.'

"The marines stood him up and said in a strange accent, 'This is your wife, understand? Do you understand, English?' Laughter.

"So, Mike and I had a good time eating and talking and watching the girls. I began to meet the real people. I got to know my friend Mike better. That couple is still married, forty years.

"Thank you all for coming." Joe sat down.

Milly stood up, "Forty-two years ago, Joe and I were in college together. We were so poor. We walked everywhere...to dances, parties, to the lake swimming. That's where he found the glass ring I have here. He proposed to me and gave me this ring. I wore it around my neck for several months.

"He said in church how childish and silly he was. Well, I feel that way now. I feel like I am nineteen again."

Laughter.

"Joe and I are together again," she continued. "But our goal is not having a family. It is to help people. Our first step to help Native Americans, starting with Joe's friends, the Navajo's. There are so many poor people, so many jobless. The government isn't doing its job. In fact, they are holding everything back. We must do everything we can to help them. It is really a quest to help them with their freedom. Such is our American Way.

"Joe and I feel your love and friendship, and we thank you. We love you back."

Clapping. There was incredible love of family all through the weekend.

Afterward at the Motel

Afterward Milly and Joe were together at the motel. Joe said, "I'm so tired, I bet I danced with a hundred people…nonstop."

Milly retorted, "More than me."

Plopping on the bed, Joe announced, "I'm asleep."

"But it's our wedding night."

"Tomorrow is another day.

"Take off your shoes."

"Ya."

"But now we're legal."

"Should I have a stroke or heart attack loving with some sweet, beautiful young thing?"

"I thought we were alone?"

"Ya, together again."

"And the Queen of England is at the door, with a donation."

"Ya?"

"And you'll give me all your money so I can run away with another man?"

"Ya, tomorrow."

"Ya I bet."

In the morning, there was loud knocking, clanging, yelling, shouting, and calling outside the motel room door. Joe went to the door. Over thirty people were there.

"Hey, Dad, come on to breakfast. Some of us have to leave town."

"Ya twenty minutes in the restaurant."

"Hey! Formal pajamas."

"Ya see you…Milly!"

"I'm almost ready," she said.

"Whoa, you're fast. Let me get in the bathroom."

"And change clothes."

Later at breakfast, there were hugs and goodbyes. Joe and Milly went home.

There was another big get-together at lunch and more hugs and good-byes. Alone.

"And now, Señor?" Milly said.

"You, me, need to get married before God," Joe said.

"That's kind of scary. Let's just hold each other a while."

Walking around the house, Joe said, "What a letdown."

"Ya."

Joe said, "So many people, so many days, so much excitement, so many kids playing and arguing—how silent, just you and me. Let's go to the bathroom and kiss for a while. Maybe I can remember how to do it."

"Si, Señor," Milly said.

"That reminds me," Joe said. "Is there any way we could set up a couple factories across the border? Then we could inch up the pay scale for the workers. It's too low now."

"Not without more money. Right now, I project a five-million-dollar shortage in two years. So, we get money or slow down, we don't grow."

"So, we pray for a way."

"It always works."

"Any firm offers on the house?"

"Getting close."

"That's a relief. Get rid of everything."

"That's scary, working for so many years for retirement, and then giving it all away."

"Ya we can be poor together."
"We could lose a few pounds."
"We'll go for a walk later."
Kissing. "Ya, we need to practice."
There was that funny giggling laugh they have together.

My Friend

I'm putting this letter here out of place because it is so important to me. I carry it in my wallet in a plastic baggie.

To my best friend Mike,

    I am writing this on our plane to Rome. We have an idea of what's going to happen but no details. We'll have to roll with the punches.

    Milly and I miss you already. You and I have been friends for over forty-five years. Can you believe it? The things we've been through, like the loss of our wives, your children, and on and on.

    This is like losing an arm and a leg. You are gone, but you are still with me. Another great loss in our lives. I have no words for this affection for my best friend.

    At the wedding you heard me talk about the love of God and mankind. I have seen you work endless hours for the company. You have shown a great love *for the people*, your wife's people.

    Then I remember your words, "How can I love God? A bearded old man and his crusading son? Then that third unknown? I can't love a man. How can I love God?"

    I had no answer for you then, your dislike for *them gays*.

    But now I have an answer. That *unknown* has talked to Milly and me. She is a wonderful Mother. I could describe her love for all of us.

    I wish you could see her, to love her too. She is God; to love her is to love God. To love her is to fulfill Christ's words.

Then I could find my old friend a happy man again. I remember your youthful love. And I remember your silliness. I remember you playing with your children.

Remember that love, remember our affection, then remember the Holy Spirit, the Mother of all love, is only a few words away.

Your friend,
Joe

The Working Honeymoon

Alone together at one office, Milly said, "You have a tear in your eye, thinking again?"

"Ya of Anna. I miss her so much," Joe said.

"I know the feeling."

"How can I love her so much?" Joe said. "Love you so much, love God so much, love so many people so much? What a mixture of happiness."

"It's a real honeymoon, not a youthful one," she said.

"Sure is."

"But happiness is short."

"Ya. Back to meeting the obnoxious people trying to cheat us; back to seeing the neighbor I want to hate, but Christ said I must love," Joe said. "What a nasty couple they are, sneaky, screaming kids, messy yard, loud music."

"Good thing we're selling the house," Milly said.

"Ya. But how do I love people like that? How can Christ tell us such a thing? All I want to do is get away from them."

"So, it seems," she said.

"And these businessmen get an extra hundred dollars here, an extra thousand here," he said. "It's a big game of cheat your neighbor. Yet they say they are Christian. They brag, 'I never get caught.'"

"I know, I deal with bad checks, late payments, broken promises every day," said Milly.

"I can't understand it. I don't…I can't do it. And God has always taken care of me. I have done well," he said.

"God has taken care of you very well…healthy, wealthy and wise," she said.

"Thanks, but what do I do?" Joe asked.

"The Bible... 'Live that people will know you are a Christian.'"

"I do. I try."

"My secret ... I try to let my love, my love for you, my children, God, everything, cover my feelings, my bad feelings. I show respect for those evil so-and-sos," she said.

"And you don't call them names?"

"Of course not," she said.

"But you still vent your anger?" Joe said.

"Privately."

"I guess I sort of do that too."

"I think so."

"And how long does my heart stay so full of love?"

"Just don't even think about it."

Everyone says it is Joe's business, but Milly and I are equal partners. In fact, Milly is a miracle worker. She runs the business. She coordinates the different departments. She deals with the various factories. She follows the money around.

Joe tells me, "Mike, such and such a chapter has called and wants a factory. They have ninety percent unemployment in that area. The people are poor. Their prestudy is nonsense, of course, but here, read it. Go get the facts. See what's possible."

"But we don't have any money. This is a lousy way to run a business. We get a factory going and making money and you give it away. How do we survive?"

"The people need the pride of ownership and success."

"So, do we."

"But we've been there...I'll sell the rest of my stock and house. We'll get the money together."

"But you have to retire someday."

"I didn't read that in the Bible."

"You always come up with some answer like that or 'God will provide.'"

"Doesn't he?"

No answer.

I like being outside the office, meeting the Navajo's, starting factories, helping businessmen. But Joe is out more than me. He travels about the world buying and selling. Trying to get donations, meeting politicians and officials. He is the one the world relates to. He says he's fed up doing it. But it must be done.

I say, "I'm getting too old for this."

Joe says, "We've only begun."

In the Living Room

"I'm going to get my hair cut," Milly said.

"Not too short...please," said Joe.

"You're in the Bible again."

"Ya this Adam and Eve story makes a lot more sense if you realize there's a million people out there—outside the garden."

"Oh...at the wedding they read, 'Adam named all the animals and plants.'"

"Like the toddler learning to talk, a language useless to anyone," said Joe.

"Except the Mother," she said.

"Ya except God."

"And?" she said.

"Would they feel naked if they hadn't seen other clothed people?" he said.

"Probably not."

Joe said, "Here, let me read what Cain says, 'I must avoid your presence and become a restless wanderer on the earth; anyone may kill me at sight.' Then God says 'If anyone kills Cain'—and on and on. Then, 'Cain had relations with his wife.' Who's that? See, there are other people around."

"It would make sense," Milly said. "So, you're on the side of the anthropologists."

"There's an answer in between," he said.

"Then why did God create Adam and Eve?"

"Like a farmer brings in a prize bull," Joe said. "Probably other reasons too."

"Another theory?" she asked.

"I've got to put it all together."

"At least you're not getting in trouble...the grass needs cutting," she said.

"But your hair doesn't."

"See you later," she said.

Joe's First Wife

"Milly, I should talk about my wife…my first wife," Joe said.

"You don't have to," she said.

"Ya the song, 'And Nothing Else Matters' but this is different. You know I met her while I was in the army."

"Sure."

"When we met, we seemed to already know each other, we seemed to be waiting…getting ready to meet each other," he said.

"How?" Milly asked.

"I thought about that. I prayed about it many years. I finally came up with the answer, maybe it was self-hypnosis. Maybe it was revealed to me. I don't know."

"And?"

"When I was younger, I'd get these terrible headaches every once in a while. It was a shooting pain from here on the top of my head into the center of the cortex. It burned even though my body was very cold. A CAT scan didn't show anything, so they gave me pain pills. I vomited so deeply. I stayed in a dark room and meditated to help ease the pain, about a day and a half."

"You don't have them anymore?"

"No, not since I found out why…in my former life…I had been shot there, in the top upper part of my head…right here." He pointed to his head.

"Dead?"

"Ya, I had been tortured first. But I didn't know the answers."

"To?"

"I was a priest. I spoke out against the German Nazis. Maybe I was part of the resistance. But no, I was just against the evil I saw…I was, in a way, a martyr. There in the pre-heaven, I had some status."

"You remember this?" she said.

"Vaguely. Anyway, in that turnaround area for being reborn, I asked a special favor. I wanted to marry a certain woman, to give her a nice clean normal life; to show her the love and concern she had missed before. I had sinned. I had used her."

"This is beyond me, but it must be your first wife?" Milly said.

"Yes, it was a planned marriage, right there in the pre-heaven."

"Go on."

"So, I was assigned to a German-speaking mother here in America. It was a nice, but rough time growing up," Joe said. "I was bounced around here and there, woman to woman, peace and strife. Giving in to the army is like giving up freedom and personal life. But I was being trained to marry her."

"And I was part of that training?"

"Yes, to know love, to know loss, to learn to love, to love with control of myself, to be ready for her threats of divorce…and the loss of her and my children. It was her club. I had been there before."

"So, you used me too?"

"In reality yes, but I didn't know, it wasn't on purpose. Life was just flowing painfully."

"So, you had sex with her before?" Milly asked.

"We were both virgins that first time…at least in this life."

"And your last?"

"Well, I was a priest, but I don't know," Joe said. "I didn't go into that life too deeply. I'm afraid to relive the torture."

"Was I there?"

"Maybe my sister. I loved her very much. But I could never go back to Germany. I'm afraid I could remember the torture."

"And the headache?"

"I guess it just disappeared," he said. "Maybe because I realized what was causing it, a bullet hole in my head. But it wasn't there anymore."

"A weird story," Milly said. "Did you tell the doctor?"

"I never went back. Then he retired."

"And you really believe this?"

"But it answers so many things that have happened in my life."

"Like?"

"Many things. Like why did the army station me in Arizona during war time and keep me here? To meet her? Why did I meet her on that day and time, and was I ready? I mean hungry for love. I had just experienced a no-touch sort of love with another woman. But the bubble burst so easy."

"What happened to her?" Milly said.

"She yelled at me and pushed me away. I broke it off. She drove off back east to Mama."

"And more women?"

"Yes, and we're not talking about them," he said.

"Ya is there more? Is this a confession? So, you served your time? For your punishment...that past life?" Milly said.

"I guess I did. Then I was allowed to marry for love."

"And your story in church?" Milly said.

"They both should be true."

"If you say so. Do you believe God or someone up there directed your life this way, even at your own request?"

"I could probably write down a hundred things that have happened to me...To show it's true."

"And you still had free will?" Milly asked.

"Who knows," Joe answered. "It seemed like it."

"And what did your wife say?"

"She too prepared herself to meet me. She went to a Catholic girls' school and learned English so she could talk to me. That whole thing was very difficult. She was born middle-class, so we thought the same way. She was smart enough and good looking enough for me. She was free and ready to get married. She had even seen me around before."

"All coincidence?" she said.

"Too much coincidence is proof in a court of law," he said.

"Just to be contrary, I won't believe you."

"OK. We just won't even talk again."

"As you wish," Milly said. "I think you have too much time to think about all that stuff and not all the work you promised to do."

"Oh, yeah," he said. "Paint the master bedroom."

"And clean the yard, fix the fence."

"Make a list."

Together Again

Mike, Joe, and Milly were talking. "Someday when I write your story," I said. "I want to tell how you got back together again."

"Well, it was my doing," Milly said. "I missed Joe."

"Don't talk like there's blame," Joe said.

"No blame, just thank you God," she said.

"Could you tell me?" Mike said.

"No secret," Milly said "After my husband died, I started thinking about Joe. I found his home in a businessmen's directory. I called his home and after a few days a housecleaner answered. We talked, and I found that Joe's wife had died a few months before. I called Joe's business, the Fund, and asked for a job interview. The secretary said they weren't hiring as they were short on funds at the moment. I said I didn't care about pay, so I was given an interview date."

"So, you knew she was coming?" Mike asked.

"She used her formal name and married last name," Joe said. "I was speechless when she came in my office, a big dummy."

"And you?" Mike asked Milly.

"I wasn't quite so shocked. Only that he had matured—gray hair, heavier... but still Joe."

"I stammered when I shook her hand," Joe said.

"Love at first sight," Mike said.

"Remembered love," Joe said.

"Shaky knees and all," Milly said.

Mike said, "I remember meeting later. You took over the business. I couldn't believe your expertise. You worked magic on all of us. The business took off."

"Thanks," Milly said, "but you two had done the groundwork."

Mike said, "Joe...I see you pull out a card and read it once in a while."

"Milly typed it for me...a reminder...it's an Epistle of St. Paul."

"About?" Mike asked.

"Basically, it says to love God above all else—wife, family, everything. When I heard it read in mass several years ago, my life clicked. I could see how God was moving me about during my life."

"Like chess?" Mike asked.

"Like a six-billion-person chess game," Joe said. "But we have the ability to resist his moves. We can each play our own game also."

"Confusing," Mike said. "So, you have said you were walking the line defying God. According to St. Paul this is great sin—the obsession you had with Milly. God punished you for your great sin?"

"I suppose so...excuse me," Joe said, walking away.

A minute passed before Mike said, "I made him mad at me."

"Don't worry," Milly said. "He'll forget it. You know him."

"It's been almost forty years, but you've changed him—renewed, energized," Mike said.

"I can't believe his love," she said. "So overwhelming."

"Controlling? Overpowering?" Mike asked.

"No," she said. "Intense, real, honest."

"Do you know why you left him forty-some years ago?" Mike asked.

"I wasn't mature enough to handle that kind of love," she said. "It could become controlling. I wanted freedom. I wanted to be my own woman. After all I had a college degree. Rare in those days."

"And?"

"Well, he became like a slave, utter devotion," she said. "I couldn't stand it."

"And you kept studying and working?"

"Through all the kids and troubles," she said. "I could never be sure my husband would stay with me."

"And Joe?"

"Never a doubt," she said.

"You have given up all these millions of dollars—even high paying jobs," Mike said. "You work for nothing...why?"

"Ask yourself," Milly said. "All my needs have been filled. I want to help others, but mostly I want to be with Joe. I need nothing but him. I need only to take care of him."

"A riches to rags story?"

"Not yet," she said. "Plus, we have the reward of such a good friend like you."

"Ya...see you later."

Mike thought, I just couldn't say I felt the same way about them too.

Native American Employment

At an informal board meeting of the Fund for the Employment of Native Americans, Mike made a small point of discussion. "Pepsi donated $2,000 and will donate another $5,000 if we let them set up machines in each of our factories, exclusively. They deliver to our Flag Dock. We distribute cans and collect money. I say that we sell for a quarter a can for morale purposes. We'll break even and pay for delivery truck fuel. They'll give us one 1 percent extra tip for the company picnic."

"Who handles the cash?" Joe said. "Insurance doesn't cover cash."

"It would be our petty cash person," Mike said. "The system is set up."

"An informal contract is appropriate," the lawyer said. "Get a time limit for exclusiveness."

"If there's no objection, let's go on," Joe said. "Milly, cash situation?"

"We are running eight days behind in paying our bills, a slight improvement," she said. "This nonprofit corporation situation needs improving. We can't cut corners anymore. But the money is in the books. But as I tell Joe, we can't expand at the moment."

"But I just talked to another company," Joe said. "They will provide the machinery, the training, set-up cash, a three-year purchase contract. An equivalent one medium-sized factory deal. We can't lose this one. We need it. The people need it."

"I already have a tribal building deal prepared for someone else that delayed on us," Mike said. "We can put them in there. But money? You know we need start-up money."

"I guess I hit the road again," Joe said. "Donations are getting hard to get. We have to get more profit somewhere."

"Then stay at home and study the whole situation," Milly said. "You need a break."

"After next week's trip, I'll take a month break," Joe said. "Any more discussion on hand?"

"Then I presume we go ahead with this new company?" Mike asked.

"Sorry," Joe said. "Yes, go ahead. Is there any discussion…No?…Then I will try to find money somewhere. See you all in ten days."

Late Afternoon Office Check In

"Dreaming again?" Mike asked Joe.

"Thinking about the old days...when we first met...all the places we went...even the prostitute houses in Mexico you took me to."

"Trying to shake your depression," Mike said.

"Ya."

"But you wouldn't go back with them, and you wouldn't let me," Mike said.

"I had a rope around your neck?" Joe said.

"Force of words," Mike said. "You sat there paying them five dollars to talk, tell their life stories, listening to their problems."

"Ya you should be thankful," Joe said. "You wanted to be writer. You need other viewpoints...other..."

"I could have gotten them out back," Mike said.

"There are too many out-back stories already."

"Now days," Mike said. "Right...but the connection is strange."

"How?"

"You were drafted into the army," Mike said. "Three years later you came back to see me. You were married...married to one of their sisters from the other side of town."

"The poor little rich girl."

"With you as her slave," Mike said.

"Joint venture," Joe said. "Spare time only."

"Not from my viewpoint."

"About Anna," Joe said. "I must apologize. I mean her prejudice against Indians. It kept us apart...our wives with their little war."

"I know," Mike said.

"And you, losing them all," Joe said. "Everyone killed. Such tragedy. So, little I could do."

"You were there for me... Thanks."

"Ya," Joe said. "You mean the Fund?"

"Ya," Mike said. "I can at least help my wife's people."

"Dedication."

"Sure," Mike said. "Milly's gone early?"

"Getting presents for grandchildren," Joe said. "She has twice as many now. You're coming to the party Saturday?"

"For your beer and steak, anytime," Mike said.

"Do the kids bother you? I mean, missing your own kids?"

"I don't relate," Mike said. "They are different."

"Milly's cousin will be there."

"Another woman," Mike said. "No thanks."

Deacon Joe at the Home of Pedro Hernandez

Deacon Joe arrived at the small home of Pedro Hernandez. He knocked and entered. Pedro was lying in the bed.

"Joe, me compadre," Pedro said.

"Pedro, my friend. I did not know you were sick. I've been traveling so much lately."

"Si. We didn't see you at church lately."

"I saw your name on the list," Joe said. "I brought you communion. Are you going to be all right?"

"No, my wife appeared to me," Pedro said. "She visits the Holy Lady every day. I will join them soon."

"Guadalupe? Such a warm wonderful woman. A real saint."

"Si. The Holy Lady comforted her—right here," Pedro said. "She was screaming in pain just before she died."

"The Lady of Guadalupe was here? You didn't tell the church—tell the world?" Joe said.

"But where would I live?" Pedro said. "They would tear down my house and build a church. We already have a Guadalupe church."

"You're right."

"And she is with us everywhere anyway," Pedro said. "Why lose my home, my memory of wife and children?"

"What will Guadalupe church do without you fixing it all the time?"

"Si…But it is you, Señor Joe? You have the eyes. You see. You say, 'See this rotten wood? This is the way to fix it.' I do it. You say, 'This wall will fall down.' I do not see that; we fix it slowly."

"And you had the patience to spend two hundred hours on that wall," Joe said. "I cannot do that."

"And I love that church," Pedro said. "It is named after our Holy Lady and after my wife."

"Ya…and what about your sons?" Joe asked.

"I tell them to dig the hole for my grave by Guadalupe. Like I dig for my father. They say that is bad luck to dig before I am dead."

"Luck?"

"I scold them; life is not luck. Look at Señor Joe. He works hard, he goes to college, he fights for our country. He helps the poor. Now he helps the poor Indians. Be a great man like Señor Joe."

"But I did not fight in the war," Joe said.

"The lady protected you," Pedro said. "But you are still a real man."

"Thank you, my friend. And you should be proud. Your sons have all graduated from college and have good jobs. You should be proud."

"Si," said Pedro. "They listen to me. They listen to you."

"Ya…and your wife is here?"

"No. But there is mí mamá. Do you see her up there? Above the door?"

"No, but I feel her love," Joe said.

"Sí. She had so much love in her heart."

"I almost forgot your communion," Joe said. "Receive the body and the blood of Christ."

"Amen."

"Finish the wine," Joe said. "You are my last visit today."

"Gracias…a thousand times gracias, Señor Joe. You have made my life more worthwhile."

"I feel the same way about you, Pedro. Say hi to the Lady for me...and to the wife."

Laughing, "Sí, Señor."

"See you next week," Joe said.

"Maybe, no."

Joe Quotes

"OK," Mike said. "Give me another one of your famous quotes or sayings."

"How about this one!" Joe said. "Time spent in the arms of your lover is not taken off your allotted time on earth!"

"Great! What if I never let go?"

"Then you starve to death," Joe said.

"Then my allotted time is over."

"Excess always has consequence," Joe said.

"You've said that many times."

"You led me there."

"Ya," Mike said. "See you later."

"Four o'clock?"

"Right."

Appearance of the Holy Spirit

The Holy Spirit appeared to us. She spoke these words for all of us:

I am the one you call the Holy Spirit.
I am God.
God is with me.
God is by me.
We sing as one.
I am here before and after time.
I am the Mother of love.
God hears no words without love.
Without love there is no salvation.
Without love, you are noise.
Evil, power, and pride thwart love.
Anger, jealousy, and sin thwart love.
Billions will end without love.
Will you follow the word of Jesus, with love?
God loves you.
But you will be judged.
I am the Mother of love.
<u>Talk</u> to me.

Joe's Letter to Milly

Mike found this letter in Milly's desk after they left. They had left so fast.

Milly, my love, my best friend.

When I am gone, I still feel you here in my arms. I close my eyes and still see your face. No wrinkles, no lines, no marks. Your beauty spot is much bigger, but still a beauty spot, a place in my memory.

To snuggle in your arms is peace and a feeling of reverence. I cannot imagine this feeling of love being a hundred times greater when we are in heaven together.

When you asked me to forgive you for leaving me, I laughed. You laughed at me. I immediately forgot those forty years. Your smile and your touch made my youth again. Didn't I act silly again? A silly old man.

And you returned with your youthful giggle. That sound circulates around my whole mind. You are my love. To know your care for me is my greatest joy. You are always waiting for my return. I am always waiting for your embrace.

This creaky old man belongs to you. Dear God, help my woman.

Love,
Joe

Author's Notes

We will all ask, and I'm sure the whole world asks, how Joe was made Pope. It is beyond belief. A small-town man, not even a priest—just a deacon. And a standby deacon at that. Joe was always on the run about the world.

Sure, he made large donations to the bishop in Gallup and Phoenix for the local missions. But they did not vote for pope.

He had met three cardinals on his travels. But why are there so many?

I can only conclude that it was our company booklet. Joe was proud of our accomplishment. It worked, so others could copy our plan. We had a fancy booklet made up, printed in several languages, and sent out to every official, religious or civil, around the world. Joe had his picture all through the booklet.

Then we sent out several hundred videos to requesters. Who knows WHO saw those?

Joe's answer to the question, "The Holy Spirit," was so simple, so unbelievable.

So, we watched the news of the death and funeral of the former pope. Then the meeting of the Cardinals.

A Bishop in Rome called Joe. "Come to Rome immediately—tomorrow. Tell us about your company. We want to know."

Joe already knew why he was going. He and Milly were packed and then left within hours. Joe's name had already been voted on and had the required number of votes to be pope.

They were met at the airport. Joe was escorted into the meeting of cardinals.

There stood our company CEO, a former army officer—outgoing, American, a lowly deacon. He had something to sell, and he knew fear was a salesman's worst enemy. Yet he spoke with great respect.

There were hours of questions—first about the company, then religious masters, then the Holy Spirit. The cardinals believed Joe. He is a top salesman. "Sell yourself, the product will be easy," he always says to us.

Joe had been voted on, but there was a motion on the floor for a revote.

One cardinal said, "I was visited in my dream by the beautiful lady. She said to vote for Joseph. But I didn't know him. Was this the Holy Spirit?"

"Any others?" Joe said.

"And I, and I, and I," around the room, "Not I."

Joe thought, Glutton. Joe reads personalities.

"Not I."

Joe thought, Just like a woman.

"Not I."

Joe thought, Unnatural lust.

And so around the room..."and I."

"Most of you have just revoted for me," Joe said.

The cardinal who had called for a revote said, "I withdraw my motion."

The cardinals clapped; they had a new pope. Let the ceremonies begin.

As Joe was being dressed for the ceremony and presentation, he commented to Milly, "These vestments are so hot. We'll have to get an air-conditioner installed later."

Milly said," I hope you used antiperspirant."

"What a thing to say to the pope."

"You...a pope?" she said. "What does that make me? Your mistress? Are we still married?"

"I suppose, like a president, you'd be a first lady."

"But I have no fancy dress, no ball gown."

"I don't suppose there is a lot of precedent—the pope's wife. I don't expect a pope's ball or dance."

Milly was dressed in a choir gown.

"Be sure to sing nicely," he said.

She made a crooked face.

They walked out the door hand-in-hand. It seemed like a million people were clapping and yelling.

There they were again in the spotlight, holding hands in the air, smiling, and waving at everyone just like at their wedding.

Now the world was watching. They wondered, "How could this be true?"

Pope Joseph Speaks to Crowd

The newly consecrated Pope Joseph stood up to speak to the massive crowd at the Vatican.

"I have dedicated my life to the Holy Spirit," he said. "I dedicate my time as pope to the Holy Spirit, our Mother. She is with Christian people until the end of time, Christ promised.

"But Christ will be coming soon. I am to be the last pope. I will oversee the calamity of this world. But for the word of the Holy Spirit and the coming of Christ, humanity will be lost.

"Thus, we must hurry. We must speak to you, lost Christians. You must come back to the Word and love of Christ. You can no longer procrastinate… time is short. All Christians must become missionaries. We have been sloppy. We've been putting it off. Now, we must <u>rush</u> toward the end. Christ is coming. He wants a report. All of you priests, brothers and sisters wasting your time going to school, playing with life, get busy. Go out and teach the Word of Christ. Become a missionary…Cardinals and bishops, thin out your priests, send them to missions. You too teach about Christ. Forget bookwork…forget bureaucracy.

"I now ask former priests, married or not, to come here and talk to me. Become a priest again, married or not. I shall soon become a married priest. You can take over the jobs of unmarried priests so they can become missionaries.

"Women that have the background, knowledge, and dedication to be a priest. Gather here with my wife. We will start a new order of women priests.

"Seminary's rush your men out. Fill them with the Holy Spirit, teaching the words of Christ.

"Will there be time to train thousands of new priests? I don't know. We will try. Even the Holy Spirit doesn't know the exact date. Christ said, 'only the Father knows.'

"But it will be soon. We must hurry. There is no time for vacations. As for birth control, we must study all means of nonlethal birth control. We do not need babies to face the coming calamity. Read Christ's words on the end time.

"We must stop abortion. God the Father is very angry about abortion. If we do not stop it, He will smash this world with his fist. We will suffer twice as much. All nations, even the United States, must make it against the law immediately…or else! But remember, Christ taught nonviolence.

"Speaking to homosexuals and lesbians, you must stop your activity immediately. Become celibate move away from the sin cities. God shall destroy them soon. Pray for forgiveness to this great sin. Pray for strength to stop.

"Speaking to the Mafia and drug dealers and other major criminals, I hereby speak the words of Christ. 'If you forgive men's sins, they have forgiven them. If you hold them bound, they are held bound.' Thus, I hereby excommunicate you from this church, and condemn you and your families to hell. You are held bound to your sins. If you wish me to revoke this condemnation, you will stop your immoral ways, help and employ the poor, help the missionaries, reeducate prostitutes, help reverse the suffering of drug users, and clean up the foreign gang situations. It is better to enter eternity a poor man than to suffer the ravages of hell. Think of your family there with you. Each family come to me personally.

"Speaking to my Japanese friends and the country of Japan, your country has many shelves of land that will move into the ocean. Only the hand of God holds them in place. He says you must become a Christian nation or drown by the millions. These slides will wipe out life around the Pacific Ocean. Much of the land east of Mt. Fuji will be the first giant slide. There will be more destruction than all the wars of time.

"And you, our Muslim brothers, we share this one same world and one same God. We are about to be punished for our misuse of this planet. We are about to be punished for our great sins against God. You will be unfairly punished with us. We ask your forgiveness for the atrocities of the crusades and our other sins of self-importance. We must start a system of daily communication to try to avoid a senseless war that will triple our worldwide suffering and carnage.

"Will your children burn with ours or can we forgive one another?

"Speaking of witchcraft and sorcery, we must be careful. TV and movies have such nice, beautiful people as witches. We wish to confirm the Bible. This power is from the devil. He is using this seductive message to mask his intentions. He is deceiving us in many ways. See through these romantic images or visit hell with him. But the witch hunts of the Middle Ages were just as evil. So, watch out.

"And you, Europe, and the United States—you have made sin into nothing. Materialism and pornography fill your lives. You no longer read and follow the words of Christ. Renew yourself. Call on the grace of the Holy Spirit. You will suffer greatly.

"Speaking of the Holy Spirit our Mother...excuse me a minute." The pope stops to get a drink of water.

Part 2

The New Pope Continues

"We all know that our one God is made up of three persons. Each person has different duties and responsibilities. When one person acts, the others know and understand, so there is no disagreement. They are one in mind and soul.

"The Bible often refers to God in the feminine. There are ancient writings of the 'Wife of God.' In the gospel, Christ laughs at the husband-wife relationships in heaven. He says, 'It doesn't work that way in heaven.'

"I tell you here, God, the Holy Spirit is female and is our Mother. She is here in this world worrying about us and helping us. It is she who is appearing in the world—like at Fatima, Guadalupe, and hundreds of other places. She is God. She is the Holy Spirit.

"Our Virgin Mary, who we all love and respect, is not God. She does not have the power of God. It is God who we must love. We must love God with our whole heart and soul. These are the words of Christ, 'Love God with your whole heart, soul, and being.' —Mark 20:30-31

"The Holy Spirit, this beautiful, charming woman has appeared to my wife and me. This enormous power of love made us slave like. She said, 'This is why we do not always appear to humans. You need the free will to choose or reject God, to choose or reject Christ's teachings, to love or to hate your fellow man. Therefore, we hide and appear only to few people.' She said to me, 'You must warn people. Billions will suffer and die. Most of it is their own doing. Try to straighten your mess out. We love you, our children, but you have run away from God's teaching. You took pleasure from the world; now you will pay for it.'

"She said that when God the Father was making Adam and Eve, God the Son and she were the models. Two perfect human beings were made. Because

Adam and Eve sinned, God didn't make wives for their sons. Quoting Genesis, 'they married the daughters of men,' those ugly women scientists tell us about. —Genesis 6:2. Thus a new form of humanity arose. These super intelligent sons created new civilizations and cities. Yet they too rejected God and God destroyed them.

"The Bible's timeline was translated wrong, and people had forgotten because of mistakes in oral tradition. But God didn't correct it. The meaning is what is important to him.

"God destroys evil—God lets us destroy ourselves.

"It is what we are doing to ourselves and our world now. Prepare yourself.

"We will soon have a large number of martyrs in the name of Christ. Remember, he will welcome them into heaven himself.

"To fund our great missionary work, we will need a lot of money. We ask for your donations. Each bishop will support a missionary program.

"We must immediately begin selling the artwork of the Vatican and surrounding churches. Bids on specific items will be taken, advertised, and then rebid. My wife will administer this program.

"If you ask why—if you feel it is wrong, I tell you this. In a few months or a few years, soon, this land, this church, will be made barren and flattened. Not one stone standing on another for many miles.

"Is it not better that our historical artwork be somewhere else? Our holy seat will be moved elsewhere before that time. The Vatican library must be moved intact. We are taking bids. But not Europe or the United States. God says, 'You will be flattened and divided.' Not the Middle East. God says, 'You will be as a torch to heaven.'

"We already discussed Japan and the Pacific Rim. Not near any volcano or fault line. God says, 'The world will be ripped, lava will flow, and the oceans will be deepened. I am your God, and you have angered me.'

"And now let us conclude with a prayer.

"O Holy Spirit, you are our Mother, please help us in the upcoming world upheaval. If we are to die, meet us with your loving embrace. Give us courage to stand up to detractors and bullies. Give us knowledge to see those that will deceive us in your name. Help us endure the suffering, the hunger, the disease, the cold and heat, the loss of our loved ones and the breath of life.

"We ask your forgiveness in the name of God our Father, God the Son, God the Holy Spirit our Mother. Amen."

The crowd claps but is quite solemn.

The Next Sunday's Sermon

"When the Holy Spirit appeared to us, she was so friendly and motherly. She was in no way superior or uppity. That is, of course, since God cannot sin. She is the sinless one.

"It was she who appeared to our Virgin Mary and implanted the soul of Christ in her womb. The Holy Spirit and the Virgin Mary are best friends, even today.

"Christ lowered himself to become human. As a human, He had no godly power. He could even possibly sin because he was like us. But he prayed to his fellow God-Person. She kept him straight and sinless. She gave him the power of miracles. She gave him the words of his great sermons. She gave him the courage to suffer and die for our sins.

"Read the Bible with this insight. God, the Holy Spirit, constantly guided Christ. He needed it. He was really human like us. He had daily temptations like us—sins of the flesh, sins of the Devil's taunts. The Devil especially picked him. He knew Christ was vulnerable. Read that in the Bible. Read the Bible every day. The mass readings are not enough for true faith and love of Christ and the Holy Spirit. Set aside time every day. Read the Bible with love, read for knowledge, and ask the Holy Spirit for insight.

"Begin talking to the Holy Spirit. Do it like Christ did. She will become your best friend too. She will guide you when temptation comes around. She will fill you with love...of God and humankind. She is the Mother of love. She is the source. She is the center of all love, human and Godlike love.

"And you, young people, your heart is crying out for love. 'Looking for love in all the wrong places.' Go to the source. Go to the Mother of love. Love to find a spouse, love to serve the church, love to fill your aching heart, and love to serve God in your own way.

"And you with aching bodies, aching hearts, and betrayed souls...who can help you? Who helped the human Christ? The Holy Spirit. She helps everyone who asks with love. Love is her password. Her true deep-down love will help your aches. She will give more love to you. And while you will find this love a miracle in itself, sometimes she helps the body pains also. She cures people every day. Yes, even today.

"Keep in mind, while we are currently in a body of flesh, we are but moments away from a life of the spirit. It is a vastness as big as space. It is different as can be. But it is our true home, our true form. We will be like that for eternity.

"If we suffer here on earth, if we are to be tortured and put to death, it is but a few moments of eternity. Think like the early Christian martyrs. 'I will suffer awhile. I may be stripped naked and devoured by an animal. I will be embarrassed in every way. My body will be desecrated. But I will continue to love God. I will suffer this moment because I will live with Christ in a little while.'

Newspaper and TV Interview

Joe and Milly are sitting on a beautiful antique sofa in a large room with about forty interviewers.

"Pope Joseph, there was a recent assassination attempt on your life. Can you tell us about the man?"

"He belongs to two different hate groups. Because I said I would be the last pope, he thought he could hurt the church. But the Holy Spirit was with me."

"And the wounded guards?"

"One dead, the other should make it," Joe said.

"And the other threats on your life?"

"Anger from many directions, especially the criminals. But if I die, who will reinstate them?"

"Some people fear the United States government will control you?"

"Only the Holy Spirit directs me. But I pray for the welfare of the U.S., especially where my children and grandchildren are."

"You have reversed the church's stand against birth control. Please comment."

"When the Holy Spirit gave me brief glimpses of the future," Joe said. "There were no children at the coming of Christ. There was one scene, real or symbolic, where enemy soldiers were roasting and eating a human baby. Such was the state of their starvation. Plus, what Christ says in the Bible, I concluded we don't need more babies for awhile. They will only be born to suffer terribly and die."

"Then you saw the future?"

"Only parts. I almost stopped breathing as it was. We will suffer."

"And Rome?"

"Four large H bombs, trying to get me at home. But we escape."

"To where?"

"Shall I tell them where to put the fifth bomb?"

"What did you tell your children?"

"I just reworded what I already stated before."

"Then we will all die?"

"Many millions will see Christ coming."

"And you and your wife?"

"I don't know...maybe."

"And the future of Japan?"

"I don't know any more than I already commented on. There is much anger there on my comment on it becoming a Christian country. We must pray for them. We must all dig deep in our hearts and forgive each other for the atrocities of World War II.

"Many on both sides still feel this great hate. It must be forgiven and forgotten.

"My words were from God. I didn't make them up."

"Pope Joseph, you inferred there were civilizations before the Egyptians, with Adam and Eve's children. Is this true?"

"I only know what I was told. Look and maybe you will find but look deeper."

"But why should we...if the world is coming to an end? If most of us will soon die?"

"Scholars die every day, looking for the answers of God's creation. Then they find what they want to know."

"You have sold so much of the Vatican furniture, but not that sofa."

"No bids yet. But it is for sale. Come and look at it later. It is very old."

"Have many criminals have come to see you yet? And, how can you deal with such sinners?"

"Some have come and begun their program of renewal and forgiveness. Christ sat down with the rich, with sinners, with the poor and diseased. Can't I?"

"A question for the first lady. How are things going? Do you have regular duties?"

"Both my husband and I are still learning and trying to fit in. This isn't a regular business. It's a country. And there is so much tradition and so many warehouses and so many people to relate to. What a job. People wonder why things take so long around here. They have no idea of the massive amount of work that goes on here—and so much variety. And now Joe has more projects for us. We must also speed everything up."

"And matters like annulment and other personal matters?"

"Nothing has changed over there yet," Milly said. "That reminds me of that joke, 'They're so slow, the world will end, and we'll still be married.' That may be a true statement now."

"Then you're taking an active role?"

"So far observing, learning, questioning procedures, making suggestions, and working on new projects—we brought in help for suggestions to speed up work. Joe is taking priests away from our workers, so we have a big change of personnel problem. But we're getting there."

"Then you are the pope's closest adviser?"

"Joe used to say about us, one and one make three concerning our working together. But we have many, many advisors, and aides."

"And women priests?"

"We have set up an individualized training program, concentrated...over two hundred women from all over the world. Some are ready to be ordained by the pope here at the Vatican. They are called the servants of the Holy Spirit. She is their cause and reason for being priests."

"Will women priests marry?"

"No. They will take the vow of chastity. They voted on it. They are quite democratic. They are primarily a missionary group. They need more members. There are over five hundred names on a preparatory list. There is so much dedication."

"What about married priests?"

"Returning priests, married or not, are carefully screened and questioned. We don't need active felons for priests. A large committee of bishops, laymen and retired priests have set up a standardized reorientation program at seminaries. Several thousand are in the program or waiting. Local bishops are handling each case individually. But each diocese sets up its own final testing jury."

"Then the church is growing?"

"Numbers mean nothing. Only faith—individual and group faith. God feels faith and love."

"Pope Joseph, do we know when the whole thing starts?"

"Read the Bible, reread my words. Prepare yourself as Christ says."

"There have been priest groups speaking against married priests, even against you being married."

"Yes, I have gone to speak to them. Many have come here. Some have deep feelings. We must pray they can accept me…I mean us."

"What did you say?"

"When the Holy Spirit appeared to us in our living room, we talked for a while. Then she blessed us both. Then she said, 'I make you, Joseph, a priest in the Catholic Church of Jesus Christ.' Then she opened my mind to theology, church history, knowledge of the Bible, philosophy, even Latin. Later here at the Vatican, several bishops and cardinals laid their hands on me and ordained me a priest. Thus, I became a priest before God and man. We are married before God and man. The Holy Spirit accepted married priests; somehow traditionalists must also do so. We need every priest we can get, even them."

"And church finances?"

"I can see Christ shaking his head and throwing up his hands, as he said: 'the poor will always be with us.' There is such a vast number of poor people in the world; the church can't do it all. Other countries must share their wealth…and to think, world upheaval has only begun."

"You already have been named. You are the anti-entertainment, the anti-rich, the anti-intellectual, the anti-big government, and the anticriminal pope. Your speeches are faith, hope, love, and charity. These nine points are like a broken record in your speeches around the world."

"I try to think of Christ speaking today. These five groups would be his pharisees. They are self-deceiving people, only thinking they are righteous. As Christ said, 'The poor, uncluttered mind, the loving, helpful person will reach heaven much easier.' A couple of years ago, I watched a minister on TV intellectualizing part of the Bible. Connecting this part to that, giving word definitions and so on. Very smart. But it was like geometry. He was not speaking the real meaning of the Bible. He was a pharisee. He was misleading the people. If we be like Christ, as the Bible says, we don't worry about silly things like eating meat on Fridays. We think of giving the meat to our hungry neighbor. So, I forgive those critics who think I should be a variety show."

"You have sold the Vatican artwork and library to help the missions. Why do more and more people keep coming here?"

"To pray."

My First Letter to the Bishops of Our Catholic Church

Greetings:

We have a serious problem in our church. I wish to clarify what I said at my consecration as the pope.

As I said, I have excommunicated the evil two-faced sinners who hide within our church. If you remember Christ driving out the sellers within the temple and of Christ and St. John the Baptist speaking against the pharisees, then you will see that I am only following their lead.

Just lately a Mafia member killed a local priest for not giving his family the sacraments. Other priests have been killed or beaten. We cannot survive this over the long-term. We must bend slightly.

Thus, I make this statement. Please tell your priests; if they are under threat of beating or death, they must give in and administer these persons. Yet these people must be warned. They must be told what I said. The grace of the sacraments is withheld until they repent and change their ways. It is my contract with God. I wish to stop their evil worldwide disruption of world peace and security. They are wrecking untold millions of people's lives.

They must come to see me for forgiveness. I will readmit them to God's order and grace. But they must stop their evil.

Please call me anytime. We are partners in our teaching of Christ's word. May God be with us.

Sincerely,
Pope Joseph

The Pope at the Pentecost Mass

"In the great distant past, before there was time, before the big bang, if that really happened, God split into three beings, each with all the knowledge and power of the first. We don't know how or why. They are three, but they are one.

"Today we remember one of the events of one of those persons who affects us personally as Christians. God, The Holy Spirit, in her hidden identity, blessed Christ's apostles with the flame of knowledge, love, and courage of Christ's teachings. It was the first day, the real beginning of Christ's church, our church. The church that the Holy Spirit has chosen me to lead into the end times.

"God is with us. Why do so few of us share this flame of the Holy Spirit? The world says it is out of style. The entertainment industry mocks us at every turn. People say they will kill us if we don't shut up. Bigger and bigger government is trying to take away our religious rights, take away our money to teach the words of Christ. Intellectual religious leaders around the world are mocking us. They say the end isn't ready to come yet. They say only a few will be chosen and taken directly to heaven.

"I tell you God has a big heart and will take who he chooses. But we must choose him first. He will read your heart, not your mind. He will not read your bank account. He will see what you have given away, with love, by the way.

"Christ said that even if you have your body burned in his name and don't do it with love, you are wasting your time.

"And let me remind some of you. You may be doing acts of love, faith, and charity out the front door but breaking the ten commandments out the back door. You are mocking Christ. You are wasting your time too.

"People are being enslaved in many ways. Humanity is being hurt. The earth is being hurt. If you are a perpetrator of injury, you will be punished by God.

"I tell everyone, pick up the flame of the Holy Spirit. Tell these people they are doing wrong. Tell them to stop. Teach them the words of Christ. Show them your great heart of love. The world will mock you, spit on you, call you names, hurt you, or kill you. But you will have that great hope of Christ. He will welcome you personally, just as he did the man hanging on the cross next to him.

"Remember Christ's words, 'I will split out the lukewarm Christian.' That means you had better spark up those flames of the Holy Spirit in your heart. There's no such thing as just squeezing into heaven. Christ must know you well.

"Remember Christ's story of the grape pickers. The owner paid them a day's wages for just an hour's work. That last hour of our time is upon us. We must pick our grapes quickly before Christ comes. We've got to get the word of Christ out to the world.

"'He who hears my words and doesn't listen will be cast into hellfire.'"

"It is everyone's duty to tell the world, not just my duty. Time is short. Christ is coming soon! Hell, fire will be a long time.

Conception

This is a conversation Mike had with Joe later when he visited him in Rome.

"I hear you're in the baby-making business now," Mike said.

"A funny way to say it," Joe said. "We only help couples. The ones that can't have a baby."

"Very successful I hear."

"We call the Holy Spirit," Joe said. "She listens to me, to us."

"The giver of life."

"Ya, I have a priest and four counselors run a weekly program, about forty couples," Joe said. "I'm getting to think many conception problems are psychological problems."

"Tell me," Mike said.

"We know a man can conceptionally control his sperm count, for example."

"And?"

"Another example, a Japanese couple, a beautiful couple," Joe said. "A good Catholic girl made to marry outside the church, a traditional wedding. I think she felt so guilty she couldn't conceive, psychological control."

"And?"

"They went through the marriage encounter program," Joe said. "He learned about the church and signed papers saying the children would be raised Catholic. I remarried them. We went through the final ceremony. Three months later we got a letter saying she was pregnant."

"Its sounds like you're taking the miracle out of your ceremony," Mike said.

"Ah...we consider each conception a miracle, an act of God."

"Ya."

"It's what makes abortion so terrible," Joe said. "Abortion is a direct insult to God."

"No commandment about that."

"Implied only," Joe said. "Like the U.S. Constitution implies so many things but doesn't directly say it. So, it puts new problems into the legal unknown. We should thank God."

"Tell me about the final ceremony," Mike said.

"After we receive communion, we stand around the table in a spiral, holding hands. The priest in the middle holds the body and blood of Christ. Milly and I are in the middle. Each person looks into their lover's eyes, and I ask the Holy Spirit to give them a baby. I deeply implore Her, if it is Her will. If it is possible. It's like we broadcast a request of love. Later I lay my hands on their hands and bless them."

"Beautiful...but I sort of worry about Milly," Mike said.

"No, she had a hysterectomy several years ago."

"That would stop God?"

"I'd better be careful how I word my imploring."

"Ya. I would think you'd have a thousand of couples trying to get in the program."

"We don't advertise," Joe said.

Later Mike asked Joe. "What's another important thing you say to the couples?"

"I tell you guys, right after sex, joke or tease your lover. It may cause an orgasm."

"And?"

"And orgasm during the time of fertility can open passages and move the sperm along," Joe said.

"You speak from experience."

"Ya, my joking tease caused Milly to have the biggest orgasm she'd ever had."

"During the honeymoon?"

"Ya," Joe said. "She said twice as strong."

"And she was over sixty years old," Mike said.

"Me too...Quite a surprise."

After a pause, Mike said, "I suppose you can't tell me what you said."

"It might embarrass Milly if she found out."

"I won't say anything."

"OK. It was very dark in the bedroom. After our normal pleasant experience. I lay there on top of her, catching my breath."

"You spoke."

"In a teasing, joking, Texas accent, I said, 'Neva had sex with a black woman fore.'"

"Oh no," Mike said.

"She laughed so loud and shook. She threw me off. She choked; she shook."

"Then?"

"We laughed and giggled together."

"Why the reaction?"

"Some prejudice," Joe said. "Something in her upbringing. It doesn't matter."

"Kids again?"

"Ya."

After another pause, Mike said, "Another thing bothers me."

"Ya," Joe said.

"Later," Mike said.

Woman?

"A man came up to me and said, 'So your God is a woman?'" Joe said.

"The definition of a woman is a human female. God is not human. Is the Holy Spirit female? We must look at what we have heard and read. As you read the Bible and read what God does and says, there are different speakers. Some of their words are very feminine, soft and beautiful, loving and kind. This is the Holy Spirit talking. Some are more masculine. This is God the son or God the Father. God in all three persons is involved with humanity; God in all three persons cares about each of us, you and me.

"The Holy Spirit is the one that listens most clearly to our inner talking to God. Her love is ready for us to hold on to, grow on.

"There is one incredible story of God the Mother forming an incredible friendship with a human being. God our Mother came to a girl called Mary. She impregnated this human girl with God the Son. A miracle beyond any other, never happened before. A friendship that bound the two together forever.

"Can we form a great friendship with the Holy Spirit, our Mother? History tells us of people that have, so why not us? Ask?

"She will tell you to read and follow the teaching of God the Son. She will tell you to find evil and sin in your life and try to get rid of them. She will tell you to clear your soul. She will tell you to receive the body and blood of God the Son, deeply, privately. Speak to Him. Let love flow from your heart.

You will feel happy...and Her love."

To Mike, Joe said, "To regress...as God our Mother impregnated the Virgin Mary, so she impregnates all mothers to be. How can anyone insult God our Mother by not accepting Her Gift?"

"You are working with couples to have babies," Mike said, "yet you said we should try to slow down or stop. Remember your vision?"

"I try to forget. It's the grandfather instinct in me. It's been three years. Maybe it I'll be another ten or twenty years. It's difficult to listen to the cries of these couples."

Mike said, "It'll never happen to me, is this your excuse?"

"Guess so."

Stroll Through the Vatican Garden

Joe and Milly were walking hand-in-hand in a walled-in area of the Vatican Garden.

"Such beautiful plants and organization," Milly said.

"Yeah, a few hundred years of tradition," Joe said.

"And how long for us?"

"Who knows," he said. "Enjoy it while you can."

"I love the fountain."

"I don't see a 'No Swimming' sign," he said.

"Not today, thank you...what should I call the pope? The one that's my husband?"

"Just don't call me too late for your loving."

"You're just a dirty old man, really."

Then there was that loud whistling sound Joe knew from his army training. He had just grabbed Milly as there was a loud explosion a few yards away. Milly screamed in pain as Joe pulled her to the ground and jumped on top of her. Six more mortars slammed into the garden.

Then quiet...then the screeching tires as the truck drove away.

Guards with their machine guns jumped to the walls, but the truck was gone.

Milly, "This isn't the right time, dear."

Joe rolled off Milly as she cried out in pain again. They were both all bloody.

The maid came running in. Joe shouted, "Bring me some clothes, call the doctor, bring some water. Hurry!"

She tore off her apron and gave it to Joe. He stopped the bleeding from Milly's side.

A guard came. Joe shouted, "Bring a blanket."

The guard ran.

Another guard, pointing and shouting, said, "Your excellency. Gone."

"We know—stretcher."

"No comprende."

Joe drew a picture with his hands.

"Si, your excellency."

"Don't call me that. I am not excellent."

Milly reminded him, "He doesn't understand."

Joe told Milly, "Just take it easy."

"They messed up the garden," she said. "So much work to do."

"I hope they didn't dig up any skeletons," he said. "Too many years here."

"Skeletons in the closet, in the garden?"

"Who knows. History lies hidden here."

"I feel faint," she said. "Am I going to make it?"

"I don't see any real bad bleeding."

"Are you OK?"

"My left arm hurts," he said, "Not bad." He couldn't tell whose blood was whose. They covered Milly with a blanket.

"In your vision, did I escape this place with you? Did I make it?"

"I don't know. I know I made it to a mountainous place. I had a knot of love in my heart. Was that love of the Holy Spirit? Love of you…dead or alive? I don't know. But we will be together a million years."

"Is that all?"

They lifted Milly onto the stretcher. Mike held the apron tightly to her side as they carried her inside. The doctor came in an hour and sewed them both up. They brought Milly blood the next day.

"We must keep quiet about our injuries," Joe said. "Tell the press we're fine. They missed us."

"How did they know where we were?" she asked.

"Probably some listening device," he said. "Only those with God are safe. I will work as usual tomorrow."

"And you'll pray for me?"

"Of course."

Next Day: Milly in Bed

"Now you have a pint of a man's blood in you. That should toughen you up."

"I don't feel like dancing yet."

"I worried so much, all night," Joe said.

"I know, but you still snored," she said.

"You are my wife, my woman."

'I know… don't be silly. Oh, oh."

"What's wrong!?"

"Remember what you said at the wedding?" she asked.

"Yeah."

"Your problem with love."

"I'd better go pray in the chapel."

"Don't mention me."

"But she can feel my heart," he said.

"That's what I'm worried about."

"How can you share my love with another women?"

"But she is God—we are people."

"But I love you so deeply."

"Be careful," Milly said. "You will lose me again."

"But you are doing such a great work…God's work."

"And you must relearn your lesson," she said. "You are the pope, not me."

"And I must pray to love you less?"

"Is that what you did when you were young?"

"No, I just prayed for help. Then I worked hard. I mixed with other people."

"Then do that again. I don't want to die. I want to see Christ's coming."

"Yeah, see you later," Joe said. "Off to work."

"Careful with your arm."

"Yeah, can't let it break open and bleed. We must keep it quiet. People need hope."

"And you forgive them?"

"It didn't happen."

"You'll forgive them if I die?" Milly asked.

Thinking

Mike was thinking about what Milly said.

"Thinking?" Milly asked.

"What if God controls the whole universe with song...music...sound?" Mike asked. "It is his method."

"That's beyond me," she said. "I think that heaven is full of beautiful music, another pleasure."

"I read somewhere about that," Mike said. "But I think it goes beyond that."

"You're talking to the wrong person. But I think of the Father out there creating new stars, new wonders, new mysteries, having fun."

"Fun?" Mike said. "God having fun. You think so human."

"Human? That's what I am."

"Yes, thank God," he said.

"It would be my penance," Milly said. "God can call us any time. It is us that are selfish."

Sermon: Mass of Corpus Christi (World TV)

"How many hundreds of times have I said, 'This is the body of Christ. This is the blood of Christ'? Do I believe? Yes, with all my heart and soul. This is the real body and blood of Jesus Christ. The real thing. And I kneel down and thank him. I ask for his forgiveness. I ask him for help. I am humble before God.

The other day I picked up my father's prayer book and read Paul's letter to the Corinthians. I cannot understand how Protestants can read this, read the Bible, and Christ's words, and not believe this really is his body and blood. I have said this is one reason Catholics have a slightly easier way to heaven.

"Yet read Paul's letter. With the gift comes greater responsibility. If we eat and drink unworthily, we condemn ourselves. If we dance up here to communion—looking at the girls, being unprepared—we are guilty of sin, guilty of offending Christ himself. With communion goes a great blessing—direct communication with Christ or maybe the future death of our soul. Maybe that's why Protestants stay away from this belief.

"In my youth, there was a discussion if Protestants could go to heaven. This shows we did not understand the great love of God. God loves us all. God hates evil. Could Christ condemn someone who loves him and follows his ways?

"As in the story of the prodigal son, will we stay at home with God and serve him, thus earning his heaven? Will we stray off to the world and waste our talents? Will we concentrate our hearts on the love of God, will we see the world of lust, gambling, and entertainment and will we be diverted from God? Will we condone the false teaching that adultery is OK, killing is, OK?

"God is our family. God is our father, God is our mother, God is our brother. They love us so much. They will punish us, as we would punish a dog that wets on our rug. Because they love us. A hundred times more than we love that dog.

"How can we offend someone who loves us so much? How can we offend them—our family—with sin? How can we break their commandments? How can we deny them, offend them? How can we confront their love? We owe them. We owe them obedience. We owe them love in return. Are you empty of love? Find God.

"The world is going into great turmoil. We must prepare ourselves. Pray to God for courage. We know not the hour of Christ's coming. We know not the hour of our death. At any time, our body may become a billion atoms, our souls screaming toward eternity. Are you going to be met by God? Are you prepared? Now?

Notes of Mike Wyschochek, the Author

When I heard the news on TV of the attack on the pope, I called right away, but their private phone was busy. I call every week to discuss business.

Milly said later that all her children and grandchildren kept calling. She hardly got any sleep.

I faxed the papal office that I wanted to visit immediately. Joe answered by fax.

"Glad to see you any time, but I recommend you wait four weeks until I return from the South American trip. We'll have time to talk and tour. So much travel, just like the old days. Call Milly with arrival time. See you. Joe."

"Oh, sure. Call Milly."

Milly started keeping the phone off the hook so she could rest. No one knew her real condition.

When I saw her, I wanted to cry—so weak and frail. "Dirty garden. She had a terrible infection, but she' going to make it."

"And you? This being the pope is dangerous. Another close call?"

"Yeah."

"That big colored picture on the front of every newspaper," Mike said. "One hand on the woman's head, the other hand raised upward. Both of you all bloody and torn clothes. Red and white cassock. A picture of the century. The words, 'Will faith, truth, and courage prevail?'"

"The pope says, 'Only Christ's words and love will prevail.' Pretty dramatic for you."

"I was only half there," Joe said. "I had concussion."

"Oh sure," I said. "Start from the beginning."

"We were in the capital in a great plaza heading for the cathedral. A half million people waving white cloths and yelling were crowding in on us. We could barely move. I saw a big flash from a building two blocks away and a rocket heading toward us. I hit the eject button. I was thrown way up in the air. Just as the parachutes opened, the blast hit. I hit the ground really hard. Broke up the capsule I was in.

"And you?" Mike asked Joe.

"Yeah, me too. Broken arm and ribs, concussion, bruised everywhere, pain everywhere. Some men helped me back to the explosion. People screaming and burning, blood everywhere. I crawled about the debris blessing and helping people. That woman in the picture was almost dead."

"Crawling?"

"My ankles were in terrible pain. My hands and legs were cut, crawling in the glass and broken metal from the van."

"After an hour or so of this, some police helped me walk to the hospital," Joe said. "My legs were rubber."

"Walk?"

"The massive number of people crushing in on us trying to see. So many had to touch me. They felt like people were poking me. I felt like Christ carrying his cross and everyone trying to touch him, last time."

"Comparing yourself to Christ?" I said. "Getting a big head there, aren't you?"

"Yeah."

"And the guys with the rocket?"

"The people pulled them out in the street and stomped them to death."

"No I.D.?"

"Mercenaries, no known connections."

"And you still went to the mass funeral in three days?"

"Pain killers, a wheelchair, and lots of tape."

"And you asked the people to forgive those monsters and the people that hired them?" I said. "We must act like the early Christian martyrs and love and forgive their killers. I can't believe you."

"So, we must."

As we toured the Vatican—with guards of course—Joe in the wheelchair, he told me everything. What problems. But we are more than friends. I helped some, gave some suggestions, helped him answer his own questions. But his problems are out of my comprehension. He really poured his heart out to me. But we are friends.

Hell

"Mr. pope, answer my big question," Mike said. "Is there lust, desire, adultery in Hell?"

"Yes," Joe said, "But no completion, no fulfillment, no release. You suffer from terrible internal pain. You crave love and affection. There is nothing—nothing to touch."

"They can't operate for a release?"

"They might operate but not to make you feel better," Joe said.

"That's inhumane."

"Right."

"Why would God permit such a place?" Mike asked.

"What did Christ say? 'You were given the words of the prophets.' You were given the teachings of Christ. You choose your own fate."

"I don't think I want to go to hell."

"I've been telling you that a long time," Joe said.

"Ya."

On the Throne

Milly told Joe, "Remember today at six, there's a dinner send off to the new missionary group. Father Milligan will fill you in between other meetings."

"You got up early this morning," Joe said. "I wanted to love with you."

"So busy, so much to do. Can't we talk later?"

"I miss my wife, my lover. Can't we slow down?"

"We're not kids anymore," she said. "We can wait."

"You keep saying that," he said. "My heart, my arms are so empty."

"You just sit up here on this throne looking down on all these women. They're the ones bothering you.

"They only make me think of you when you were young," he said.

"You didn't know me then," said Milly. "I was so full, so healthy."

"I didn't know you when you were pregnant."

"I was beautiful. I was ugly."

"I want to hold you. Can't we go back to our room? Just a few minutes."

"You and your few minutes," she said. "It always takes you a half hour. You're getting old."

"And don't you like that half hour?

"Yes...very much."

"Well?"

"But then I'll have a hard time getting back to work," she said.

"You can find some time in the schedule? Lunch time?"

"I can say you need a nap," she said. "You didn't sleep well."

"It's the truth," he said.

"Well, OK, but just for you."

"I should hope so."

Milly laughed. "See you later."

"I can't wait."

"Concentrate," she said.

A Letter to the Bishops of Our Catholic Church

Greetings:

We should like to send this informal letter to you before our meeting of Bishops next month. There are several areas of church policy that have constantly been questioned since I came into office.

Remember, I am your servant. I am ready to see you any time, even though it may be during exercise time. So many people have so many problems. But we are all the servants of the people. But we must speak about the big problems too.

In our meeting, we must define the role of the Virgin Mary, Christ's mother. She is, of course, the closest of friends to the Holy Spirit, our real Mother. We must not offend or slight either woman. Yet we must adore only God. Yet we carry this great love of the Virgin Mary. Have we prayed a thousand rosaries?

As churchmen, we must stop being pretentious. We must stop showing signs of wealth. The Gospel tells us about Christ's dislike for pharisees. The Holy Spirit says that many of our predecessors are suffering greatly because of their earthly self-importance, gluttony, greed, and fake piety. We must all learn to be humble. Our status, our power, is from God.

In like thought, I now ordain that this Catholic church strip itself of its wealth. All the land, stocks and bonds, and bank accounts—everything that's not absolutely necessary. Slum buildings must be repaired or torn down before being sold.

We must help the poor...we must teach the poor about Christ. We must all become missionaries for Christ...around the world, down the street, next door.

Any wealth will be worthless soon as the end time approaches. Yet our Great Judge will look on the wealth of the church in disgust. Will we join our suffering predecessors? Will we tell the Great Judge we liked watching TV rather than going out helping the poor and teaching His Word?

I know that I have my foot in my mouth concerning birth control. So we must come to a common answer. I spoke from my heart, not as a churchman. But I saw future disaster.

Concerning the rush of men and women toward holy orders, we must set minimum training criteria. We need these people. Holy teachers must speak out to the world.

Concerning race relations, we must remember that our Great Judge sees our souls, not our skin color. All humans must be treated fairly and equally.

Concerning our media ads against abortion, I would like letters concerning our more positive approach and an adoption approach.

Concerning the rash of holy sightings, we must be careful. We must not offend the Holy Spirit. But there is much fakery. Perhaps even the Devil's deceptions. Souls are being led astray by broken promises, unreal cures, and useless demands. Telling a future truth over here can be a set up for the Devil's deception somewhere else.

In conclusion, I must apologize concerning some of my clumsy attempts to correct the needs of the church. I am trying...I am learning...we are all entering a time where there is no precedent. But we must try. We must hurry. May God be with us.

Sincerely,
Pope Joseph

Love

"Joe, that first meeting with Milly, you don't talk about it," Mike said.

"NO."

"Big secret?"

"NO."

"I know you weren't naughty," Mike said, "two innocent doves."

"NO."

"Then why don't you tell me?"

"Compare this," Joe said. "You walk into a room, and there sits the Holy Spirit. You see part of Her blazing beauty and glory. Could you relate that shock, that overwhelming feeling to someone?"

"That bad, huh," Mike said. "But Milly's a grandmother not a great beauty—wonderful yes, but..."

"You see her differently than me."

"Ya," said Mike. "Change the subject. You saw the Holy Spirit. How was she dressed? Do they wear clothes in heaven?"

"No real need there, but they dress up for us."

"What did she have on?"

"I might compare it to an Indian sari, but different, still shapely," Joe said.

"So, I suppose no clothes in heaven means no sex in heaven?" Mike asked.

"Possible for people with bodies, but there are a million more fun things to do."

Mike said, "I can't imagine what?"

"For example, thousands of theme parks, from real dinosaurs to rock and roll, whatever you want to see or do."

"Fun, parties, learning, enormous love, it could all get boring, monotonous," Mike said.

"No such thing in heaven," Joe answered. "Boring, lonely, suffering is on the other side of the great divide."

"That's Jesus's story."

"Makes sense to me," Joe said.

"Ya. Her voice?"

"Like a loud whispering, but mostly telepathic direct communication."

"Her looks?" asked Mike.

"We just couldn't see," Joe said. "It's like our eyes all watered up."

"Your feelings?"

"Think…that honeymoon feeling you had times five. Afterward Milly and I went into the bedroom and made love. We were physically and mentally overwhelmed."

"God watched you have sex?" Mike asked.

"Like you watch a couple bugs," Joe said. "You forget—she only relates to the great feeling of love."

"You and Milly are so lucky."

"Love and luck and not related; great love calls in the hand of the Holy Spirit. You love, she helps."

"Ya," Mike said. "I still can't believe God watched you have sex. It seems… sacrilegious."

"She is always drawn to great feelings of love," Joe said. "She is with all married lovers."

"Go on."

"She wishes she could give babies only to those people. But she must follow the God directive. After Christ's coming, she will only give a baby to married lovers."

"Wait…the God Directive?" Mike said. "What's that?"

"To let the world seem to be operating on its own. That God is not running the whole thing. She disagrees on this love-baby thing."

"This Holy Spirit disagrees with God?"

"She can disagree," Joe said. "She can have opinion. She cannot dispute herself as God. She is one."

"I don't understand," Mike said.

"Ya...I don't understand the whole thing either."

The Bishop's Inquiry

"You were called into the bishops' meeting today, without me?" Joe asked Milly.

"Very nice men, but lots of questions," she said.

"Can you tell me?"

"We started out with my work, my coordination of departments, my audits, my work with the lady priests, my methods of making sure money isn't being stolen, on, and on, for three hours."

"Then?"

"The big question," she said. "The Holy Spirit in our living room."

"I'm sure."

"Why didn't we turn our living room into a sacred place, a church?" she said. "I told them what Pedro said, 'She is everywhere: Do we need more churches?' And what about money and manpower for the churches? She makes thousands of private appearances. They understood. Many of them have seen the Lady in a dream."

"You impressed them?" Joe asked.

"Bishop Montinu made this statement, 'If we could know that a pope's wife could be this virtuous and competent, then we should recommend all popes have a wife.' What a compliment."

"Watch out for that guy," Joe said. "He has an eye for women."

"I am a one-man woman."

"Ya...you answered him?"

"I reminded him you were the last pope," she said. "Christ will be our next church leader."

"Ya but they must be thinking of your free labor, one of the best corporate money managers in the world."

"Whoa, another compliment. Too much for me...and they called you in?"

"I have to keep telling myself they're not trying to insult me," he said. "They just want to know."

"I sometimes get that feeling too," she said. "After a long discussion, they concluded today's meeting with this statement, 'Since most of us are sure, are convinced, that the Lady of Lourdes is the Virgin Mary, we must consider that both Holy Ladies are appearing to people around the world.'"

"That implies God is busy, billions of people," he said.

"God busy?"

"Think of the computer system they must have," Joe said. "Intimate facts on billions of people are beyond belief."

"God busy...I can't imagine her keeping track of billions of people...And giving personal service..." Milly said.

"That's part of the awe of the universe, the awe of God."

"Ya," she said. "I'd better rest...more questions tomorrow. The inquisition."

"But no whips. Only verbal."

Praise

We often say in church "Praise be to God." That used to be a problem for me, how do we praise someone who has everything? Like buying a gift for someone that has everything. So, I prayed with empty words, like the Holy Spirit says, "without love, without meaning, you are noise."

Mike began to praise God and thank God at the same time.

"You are such a great God, so loving and giving. I thank you a million times for your caring, for giving me so much. You give time to us; you calm my mental problems; my worry fades away. Please increase my love for you. Please help my family find your peace. Help me chase away the devil with his evil thoughts and temptations. You have that authority, that power. Thanks a million, thanks, Amen."

The Last Words of David

An interviewer asked Joe, "Pope Joseph, how can you excommunicate the drug dealers and mafia? Aren't you supposed to forgive them, accept them?"

"I remember the last words of King David in the Bible," Joe said. "'The wicked are like thorns to be cast away. We must arm yourself with iron and spear. They must be consumed by fire.'"

"Strong talk," the interviewer said.

"They have no idea how they are harming vast numbers of people. They must be told. Christ told us to warn our sinning brothers."

"You have no fear?" the interviewer asked.

"God is with me," Joseph said. "I have this deep feeling that I want to be with her."

"Her?" the interviewer said. "I can't think of God as a Her."

"Then think of God as a family, a father, a son, a mother."

Interviewer: They listen to our prayers?" the interviewer asked.

"Yes, through the Holy Spirit. She is the one that is really with us, day by day. Christ is with us through Her."

"Yes, thank you."

A Few Days Later

Milly told Joe, "I haven't seen much of you lately…lots of work?"

"Yeah."

"And your problem?" she asked.

"Yeah, life is a lot less pleasant now. But I'll recover."

"What do you mean?"

"I was given a shot of reality; the bubble burst."

"You want to talk about it?"

"I don't want to offend you in any way," he said, "so I'd better not."

"No, I need to know," Milly said.

"I saw you as dying, leaving me again, that terrible pain of separation. I had to harden my heart against that. I had to pull away."

"And?"

"That's enough, the rest is unpleasant."

"I'm not a child," she said. "Tell me."

"I saw you as an outsider would…getting old, sagging, getting wrinkles, torn flesh and blood, rough skin, getting crabby and pushy…"

"Pushy? You need it."

"Sorry."

"You make me so mad," she said. "Get out of here. Do your work. Go paint the Sistine Chapel."

"OK. I will paint shorts on the naked men."

"Yeah. The women too. But do not look at them."

Letter to Members of the Catholic Congress

Greetings:

Our first meeting is world-shaking news. The Holy Spirit is pleased, and the world is applauding. You made history.

Formal agenda and committees have been set up just like any democratic government on earth. The word of the people will rule our church.

The Holy Spirit has requested we include more women and Protestants in our congress, in both houses. Might there be *lay* cardinals in the House of Cardinals? It is your point of discussion at our next meeting next month.

The Holy Spirit said there is a similar congress in heaven. God listens to their proclamations. God is not a dictator. Heaven is joyous, meaningful, busy. Forget the concept of praying and singing all the time. She even implied there were representatives from other worlds. I wonder?

As before Father Ramone is coordinating, scheduling meetings and arrangements. I requested that he draw up a list of names of women and Protestants who may be requested to join our congress. We have formed a representative government that is world-reaching in its agenda.

Thanks be to God, Your Servant,
Pope Joseph

Questions: Why Has the Holy Ghost Hidden From Us?

Question: Why has the Holy Ghost hidden from us? In the Bible, she appears as a dove. She has not identified herself in apparitions. And why now, after so many hundred years?

Pope's Answer: God the Father is the leader in this one godhead. Each person in God has their own duties. The Holy Spirit is here with us acting as a Mother, loving us as a Mother, but needing to let us go out on our own, not ruling our lives.

Historically people made up stories of the goddess. Many cavorted. There were beauty contests, and some were nasty, and on and on. The Holy Spirit needed to remain neutral of such false stories. She is, after all, most beautiful, most intelligent, most powerful, most loving...

Then we have the long history of subjugation of women. Could a man make himself adore a God that is a woman?

Remember what I said before about Her enormous power of love. If we knew Her completely, we would be enslaved, overjoyed, enraptured. Such we will know in heaven in varying degrees.

If you remember the commandment, "Thou shalt not take the name of the Lord thy God in vain." —Exodus 20:7

Go out to workplaces, bars, wherever men gather. You will hear the commandment broken over and over. Think how ugly their comments would be if they knew God as a woman. God the father and his Son are protective of their beloved, the Holy Spirit. Would they intervene in our lives if her name is used in vain...or in filthy talk?

The Holy Spirit is appearing now to warn us of the upcoming world disaster, as a mother would warn us, more and more often. She must warn us as God, not as a former human. Christ's Mother.

We must be careful of these apparitions. The Devil might be behind some of these trying to deceive us. That great con game to twist us away from God's laws. God will not give us permission to change or break his laws. If you are told differently, it is not from God.

So we are given the free will to choose God, love and adore God, or choose to love nothing or evil. We can follow His laws, or only man's laws or only the Devil's laws. But we must choose. Remember what Christ said about warm water that he spits out. Shall God spit you out? Because you believe in nothing or only a little.

Think about St. Paul...how Christ expressed his glory to him. St. Paul could not stray even an inch from the words of Christ. Do you want that responsibility? St. Paul urges us to take that responsibility even though we have not seen Christ. Christ said, "Blessed are they that have not seen me but still follow my words." —John 20:29

We had better read them over and over.

Question: And so, the church will proclaim the worship of the Holy Spirit as our Mother?

Pope's answer: Our church is not proclaiming new issues of faith. What I said is truth. But it is not an act of faith according to the church.

Such was the decision of the bishops at our meeting. All emphasis of the Holy Catholic Church is to prepare for the end time. Such will be our formal pronouncement. We will emphasize faith, hope, love, and charity. Each of these will be tested to the highest degree in the upcoming events.

The church has proclaimed you go to church every Sunday. Does that get you to heaven? Read Christ's story about the pharisee and sinner. It might be easier for a Catholic to get to heaven, but it is not automatic. Protestants, Muslims, and Jews will go to heaven, but not all. Christ will read our hearts. I cannot speak for other religions at all.

Intellectuals and rich people will have a hard time getting to heaven. Ask yourself, "Am I acting like a pharisee? Read Christ's words about his dislike for pharisees. He will be your judge after all.

Correction

Mike stated that the Holy Spirit has been appearing to people, not Mary the mother of Jesus Christ. My advisors have corrected me. I, as a businessman understand, "delegation of authority..." The advisors have given me biblical stories of this happening. Saints or angels. So, I restate: the Holy Spirit can send Mary or saints to us to communicate, maybe warn us of the future, maybe correct our plans. This begs the question: with so many more people in the world, is God busy? No, she still listens to our hidden prayer. She still loves each of us. She is God enough. She has no limit.

So, what about those of you with a hardened heart? You had so many evil things happen in your life. You try to pray; you cannot love. Remember she said, "Without love you are noise—no salvation."

What do you do?

For most of us, love develops slowly. Several times a day talk to Her, asking for love, deep, deep down in your heart, then deep in your soul. She will begin to listen. Your love will grow, slowly. You will feel the difference quietly.

Small Meeting with Newspapermen

The newspaperman asked, "Pope Joseph, our readers are asking about your statements about Adam and Eve's sons. Can you comment on your vision?"

"I was not given a complete story," Joseph said. "I've been mentally trying to piece it together."

"Tell us more. When did it happen?"

"I would guess about four thousand to nine thousand years ago," Joseph said. "I will tell you what I think. But you must not take it as words of a pope. This is an educated guess based on revealed facts and visions of large civilizations long ago. I could not place them. I didn't get names."

The newspaperman said, "We will quote your words 'educated guess.'"

"I was told Adam and Eve had twelve sons, besides the one killed," Joseph said. "An angel educated them in the ways of the world—farming, reading the sky, math, science, building, seafaring, and the laws of God and justice. The Bible only tells us about the son that preceded Noah."

"And one brother became like Judas, killing his brother?" said the newspaperman. "You're comparing the twelve apostles?"

"Yes, God told the rest to go out and serve the world, change mankind, rule men with his commandments," Joseph said. "These men were big, handsome, highly intelligent and educated. They lived for many hundred years. One or two even went to America."

"And one maybe started Atlantis?"

"Maybe, or places like it," Joseph said. "But each brother was different. Some became traveling teachers. Some heroic fighters for justice. But they all had many children, some even thousands."

"Thousands? How?"

"As some become rulers, women were brought to them every day. Those earlier people could smell when a woman was fertile. These sons changed humanity physically."

"And morally?"

"Somewhat—hit and miss. They didn't get everywhere. Then some became corrupted by power, greed, and various sins. The Devil talked to some of them into believing themselves God. Then they felt God's wrath."

"The cities you saw were large?" asked the newspaperman.

"Some seemed endless. Others less so, different styles, some with walls, most without."

"This was before the flood?"

"Yes the flood must have really been sudden and devastating," Joseph said.

"It covered the whole world?"

"I would prefer to think of the whole world as they knew it, the Middle East. I would guess the glacial melting had something to do with it also. The oceans and Mediterranean Sea got much deeper suddenly, killing thousands. Perhaps a broken ice dam, more than just rain."

"Then some of those cities are under water?"

"Maybe melted away over thousands of years. Maybe preserved under mud and sand. I don't know. Some few men brighter than Leonardo de Vinci lived and taught, then their knowledge passed away. Perhaps some secret desert cult passed the knowledge on to the Egyptians. That would seem possible."

"So, a large Egyptian precivilization could be under the Mediterranean Sea?"

"Yes and out in the desert. It was grassland then."

"So that's your theory," the newspaperman said. "Can't you ask God for the answer?"

"Right now, I need to pray for problems of the current human race. I'll get my answers when I die."

"But that's too late."

"For a Christian, life just keeps going on. We just don't have a body hanging on. I will learn my answers. Pity the scientist who dies with questions and doesn't get to heaven. His whole existence is forever a question mark."

At a Later Sunday Sermon at the Vatican

Pope Joseph began, "I have been asked to comment on the words of the Holy Spirit. You have seen them in print.

"I am not a theologian. I am a humble priest—middle intelligence. I can only speak from my heart. I only wish to praise God. The Holy Spirit had my wife write down these words: 'I am God ... God is with me ... God is by me.'

"This is very confusing, so far, but she then answers our questions 'We sing as one.' Choir please."

The choir sings the "Alleluia Chorus."

"God sings. Heaven is joyous. We will sing with new voices with God. Our old croaking voices will sing freely and happily. Choir please."

They sing the "Alleluia Chorus" again.

"She also means that all three persons in God are together, mind and soul," Joseph said.

"Then she said words much like Christ's. 'I was here before there was time. I will be here when there is not time.'

"Of course, our one God is three persons, and they have existed before time, a block of time between forever.

"Now she says something new, 'I am the Mother of love.' Nowhere in the Bible is this stated. Yet deep in our hearts we know this is the truth. God is the center of all love in existence. This is the part of God where all love is centered. She was there at our creation as human beings. She is the center of our endearment. She is the one we must pray to. She will fill our hearts with love and fire of the Holy Spirit's power. Don't be afraid of the power.

"Then she says, 'God hears no words without love; without love there is no salvation, without love, you are noise.'

"These are much the same as Christ teaches, but from a different viewpoint, more emphasis, more clarity, and definition. Not the storytelling method of Christ. Then she hits with more strength. 'Without love, you are noise.' In other words, we are worthless piles of trash if we don't have love. 'Love of God, Love of our fellow man. Love of our earth, our people, and so on.'

"The next lines the church has always taught, 'Evil, power, and pride thwart love; anger, jealousy, and sin thwart love.' She wants to emphasize sins that especially bother her.

"Then a shocking statement, 'Billions will end without love.' That is our fault as Christians that we don't have the missionary spirit. We don't rush out and teach the words of Christ. We are losing billions of people to evil. They never learn about Christ's love. Maybe only human love, but not the real thing.

"Going on she asks, 'Will you follow the word with love?' She emphasizes that we are responsible primarily for our own soul. We must leave everyone around us if they are not for Christ. Christ said to clean our sandals and move away. Carry our teaching and love to someone more accepting, more grateful. But do the whole thing for the purpose of love.

"Then she sort of repeats herself for emphasis, 'I am the Mother of love. Without love, you are irritating noise.'

"If we do not go to this Mother, who is God. If we do not pray and beg for love, both coming and going. If we do not carry love in our hearts, all the time, every day, God does not listen to us. We are like a roaring engine going by. God will cover Her ears.

"And yet Christ says, 'We are looking for that lost sheep.' Don't ever give up. Keep praying for love. Begin small acts of kindness and work up. Become less grouchy, more friendly, more helpful, more dedicated to serving God and your fellow humans.

"We may die as sheep in the slaughter, but we will die as Christ taught us. We must be servants of God and mankind. We must love God will all our hearts. We must love mankind as we do ourselves. Then we will not be an irritating noise to God.

"Christ will know our name and shake our hand as we enter his kingdom. He'll say 'Good job, loyal servant. Go to the head of my table.'

Walking in a Large Courtyard, Guards Twenty Feet Behind

"I can't stand it here anymore," Milly said. "I'm getting out of here."

"I know the feeling," said Joe.

"It isn't safe, people trying to kill us," she said. "I miss my family. I miss home. It's not fun anymore."

"Yeah. Getting hurt takes away the enjoyment. But it's our job."

"Well, I'm leaving," Milly said.

"But you're my wife—you are my love."

"Yeah, I'll miss you. But I'll be alive; I'll have my grandchildren."

"And your lady priests? They need your guidance. You are their Frances of Assisi."

"I know, but they'll survive. They have voted a new leader."

"A very nice lady."

"And I'm going to get a face lift, a tummy tuck, a bath in Oil of Olay."

"And you're still mad at what I said?" Joe said.

"Not really."

"I don't think the church will pay for the operations."

"I don't care. I'll get an extra job at home."

"Home won't be the same either," Joe said. "The whole thing is starting."

"Yeah."

"Take a two- or three-week vacation. Get some Arizona sun and clean air. Get our children ready."

"Yeah."

"Use our Social Security savings account. Give each of our children $4,000 to stock up on food, water, warm clothes, and breathing masks. Get them ready."

"Yeah."

"I told Mike to buy large amounts of food," Joe said. "Hidden warehouses. He'll start large soup kitchens when the going gets bad."

"Talking about Mike, I am taking Lisa with me. She wants to see Mike again. They seem to really like each other."

"I noticed that. When she served us dinner, they started talking. We sort of got left out. They went out together?"

"Several times," Milly said. "She has that light in her eyes."

"Mike needs someone."

"They both do. She's been a widow for thirty years. She has worked here most of that time."

"I didn't know, but I'll pray for them."

"Then I can go?" Milly asked.

"Just don't stay too long," Joe said. "Time is getting very short."

"And if I go to Las Vegas and get a divorce?"

"There's no such thing as divorce."

"And if I run away with another man?"

"Scandal is a great sin."

"You have all the answers."

"Yeah."

"But I couldn't do that," Milly said. "You are such a great lover."

"It's my job."

The Records Via Mike

The first time I visited the Vatican, I had some free time, so I snooped around. You know me. I found there were microphones all over the place leading back to recorders. Important conversations and anything the pope was involved with were typed out and put into a historical record file.

So, I skimmed the file, stole several personal conversations. On later trips, I stole more. Many things are not church historical business. Studying these conversations helped me learn Joe and Milly's style and conversation patterns so I could piece together other bits and pieces of their new life. Here is one personal recording. Joe is alone in the Sistine chapel. It's dark—a few candles are flickering.

"Oh God, oh God, oh God, forgive me, a sinful man. This love man instinct inside me is trying to take me over. There is my wife, broken and bleeding; please help her. And I, what do I do? I search the faces of many women, looking for a new wife. Why? Why can't I think faithfully? I love you; I love her. Why can't I love faithfully? Am I really the dirty old man she called me? Yes...old man. Why would I even need another wife?

"God, if you take her, please take her into your love. Give me the strength to keep doing your work, your plan. But I plead with you to keep her by my side. She makes me whole. I do much better work.

"Could I work hard with a great slash of pain and loneliness across my heart? Would I go back into that trance when I first lost her?

"But you are God, you know best. You are ruled by the God directive. To us, this makes life unsure and unpredictable. We can't even be sure of you.

"But I know you; I love you with all my heart.

"Whatever is, whatever happens, I am your servant. Amen."

To Pray
(Sunday Sermon)

"Today let us talk to the Holy Spirit. She is listening, waiting for our smallest personal prayer. Let us parallel the 'Our Father.'

"Oh, Holy Spirit, our most sacred Mother, who is with us here on earth, hallowed and beloved is your name. When the Father's kingdom comes, you shall rule with him surrounded by a million holy women. We who adore you shall pray at your feet. Give us each day a touch of your love that we may forgive those that trespass against us. And lead us down the path of Christ's teachings, that we may live with you in heaven. Amen.

"Pray with your heart. Also pray the 'Our Father' with your heart, not just empty words, not proud pharisee words.

"You will soon read the creed with me. Do you remember these words, 'the Holy Spirit, and Lord and giver of life.' Those of you who want a child—those that can't stop having babies. Those with physical problems. Remember who to pray to, the Mother of Life—that can be physical life or spiritual life. Didn't She create life within a virgin? Maybe She will solve your problem. But do not pray selfishly. Pray for an answer. Maybe you have no children so you can serve the church full-time? Ask for her peace, her love. Ask of Her guidance.

"The Creed, 'Who spoke by the prophets.' She is as important as God the Father and God the Son, and for me, she is much easier to love. Christ said love God with your whole heart and soul. Loving the Holy Spirit counts as loving God.

"The Creed, 'She proceeds from the Father and the Son.' When I try to think of the Trinity, I think of the Father as the leader, Christ and the Holy Spirit are twins, brother, and sister, bound by enormous love. Like human twins they think and feel each other's thoughts. They share a great bond. She was there for Christ, helping him with his human self, guiding him, giving him strength. But Christ had to experience the full depth of being human. He could not carry along his godly powers and strength.

"So, you ask, 'Is God still involved with us on a daily basis as She was with Christ?'

"Yes! But we must ask; we must seek. She gets tired of knocking on empty heads. She wants your love, your fervor, your excitement. Love begets love, love begets sharing with your neighbor. Love of God means loving everyone, even that drunk in the gutter, that prostitute on the street, the starving of body and soul. Help them!

At a Private Meeting with the Pope
(Omitting Spanish and Translations)

A Swiss guard said "Presenting Señor Hazus Chavez...Señora Maria Chavez, and family."

"Welcome to the Vatican Hazus and Maria, welcome my friends," said Pope Joseph. "You have come to return to the Catholic church."

"Your honor, this is my family," said Hazuz. "The ones you condemned to hell. Even the little babies."

"Only God is our judge," Joseph said. "I only make recommendations. I have read your letter. I have talked to your bishop and priest. I have talked to your country's officials. Do you all wish to be reinstated in this Catholic church?"

"Si, we do," said Hazuz.

"Do you confess to your terrible sins against mankind and the children of God?"

"Si, we do."

"Will you, as said in the Bible, remind your brothers and sisters to stop offending God and mankind?"

"Si, we do."

"Will you continue to support the missionaries in your country and also be a missionary yourself to the people you meet?"

"Si, we do."

"Will you remember that Christ said to love your neighbor. Love is the key word. Your confession and your giving are nothing without love."

"Si, we do."

"Then I, in the name of the Holy Church, in the name of God the Father, God the Son, God the Holy Spirit our Mother, forgive you and reinstate you in their grace. Amen."

"Amen."

Pope Joseph walked among the family, joking with babies, patting children on their heads, smiling, and joking.

"But you are not such a bad man," Hazuz said, "for an Americano. We were going to have you killed…are all the drug runners condemned to hell? Even so and so and so and so?"

"Yes."

"Good."

"But you must forgive them."

"That is hard. They are evil. They are devils."

"Forget your hate; stay away from them."

"That is hard."

"God Help you."

They left. The Swiss guards came out from behind hidden places. They were well armed. No one was going to hurt their friend, their captain, their pope.

Interview Continued the Next Week

Interviewer 1: Pope Joseph, I went back and read Genesis, especially part six. I couldn't believe what was said. I must have thought it was nonsense before, sons of God having sex with human women. Were they Adam and Eve's sons? Were they superheroes?

Pope: As they told the creation story of their parents, the people considered them gods; not to mention looking at them and hearing them teach. They were big men.

Interviewer 2: I can imagine stories of Hercules and other heroes about the world.

Pope: Maybe. Oral stories could have lasted thousands of years.
Interviewer 3: I thought the sons of God were angles and certainly not Christ.

Pope: Angels don't need sex.

Interviewer 1: So great knowledge existed in the world those many thousand years ago? Knowledge of science, math, space, continents, and so on?
Pope: Yes, lost by sin, war, fire, laziness, selfish control of knowledge. We see evidence of great knowledge in the past all around the world.

Interviewer 3: About how many people were in the world at the time of Adam and Eve?

Pope: All around the world. I would guess four million.

Interviewer 2: And the garden of Eden?

Pope: After the northern glaciers melted, the climate of the Middle East changed to desert. So, the garden dried up.

Interviewer 1: And the scientists say the Sphinx is over twelve thousand years old. What happened to the people, their buildings?

Pope: The great flood covered them with mud; the Mediterranean Sea filled up and covered their cities.

Interviewer 3: What about those Christians who say there were no people before Adam and Eve; that scientific evidence is not read correctly?

Pope: Then who did Adam and Eve's children marry? God would not allow his law to be broken. I mean the one about the brothers and sisters marrying.

Interviewer 2: That reminds me—evolution theory says that modern human species developed about thirty to thirty-five thousand years ago, long before Adam and Eve.

Pope: Yes, God had that foresight. Either there was an evolutionary jump or maybe another Adam and Eve. God had to prepare husband and wives for Adam and Eve's children. It would be like us trying to marry one of those monkey people from the movie *Planet of the Apes*.

Interviewer 1: Wait a minute—you mentioned evolution? People evolved?

Pope: I think so. But what everyone doesn't consider is that God was involved. He changed things, He created new species, He exterminated species. He evolved some species; He let others stay the same; this is His world. There are hundreds of extinct species yet to be discovered.

Interviewer 2: Then you think both evolution and creation occurred. The great argument is nonsense.

Pope: We must look at the big picture from God's viewpoint. We tend to look at only what is in front of our nose. It should be a scientist's job to see what God did, then we theorize why and how.

Interviewer 1: I'd like to make another point…From Genesis—God put the mark on Cain and Cain says, "Now everyone will want to kill me," and God answers in the same way—there were people all over the world…and God concurs.

Pope: Good point—keep reading. Cain started a city. That takes thousands of people, not a few brothers and sisters.

Interviewer 3: Then why did God create Adam and Eve? If there were thousands or millions of people already?

Pope: I wonder that too. We will have to ask him. My guess is that there was a genetic weakness that needed to be straightened out. Twelve big husky sons traveling about the world do that.

Interviewer 1: Thank you, Pope Joseph, for the theory.
The pope nodded and waved goodbye.

To the Bishops of Our Catholic Church

Pope Joseph was in in a small meeting with religious leaders of many faiths from around the world—about two hundred people—God spoke to us. Each heard in his native language.

I am the Father.
He who blasphemes the Beloved, blasphemes me.
He who blasphemes the Son, blasphemes me.
Prepare for His return to your world.
Stop your evil, seek forgiveness, find love.
Care for your neighbor.
Before the judgement.
The Son will drive out the evil ones.
But you will cry; you will live with terror.
Only the Beloved can help you.
She is with you.

So as God warns us, so must we warn the people. Do not be caught unprepared; do not be caught in a state of sin. Love God, love your neighbor, forgive, and forget trespassers. Prepare your body and soul to run toward that unknown end. Those who give up are lost. Those who raise themselves up shall be lowered.

Thus I remain your humble servant.

Pope Joseph

Mike Wyschochek—The Author

I met Lisa and Milly at the Phoenix airport late in the evening. We had a pleasant meal before we left for Flagstaff.

Lisa and I were in our own world. Milly was talking. She called my name to ask me a question. I must have answered her. We two old people fell in love so easily, so fast.

Lisa had been a poor little educated widow. But years of serving the newsmakers of our world and years of reading at the Vatican library has made her a very wise woman.

I can hear her scolding, "Cardinal of the church, and you eat so sloppy." "President of your poor country, and you're as fat as a pig." "Pope of the world, and you didn't brush your teeth." She says things so funny.

It was her last night in Flagstaff, and we were embracing. I went a little crazy. She pushed me away carefully and scolded me. "Such an old guy and so many hands. You're dancing like a wild food mixer. You'd better hurry and marry me, or you'll get me in trouble."

I calmed down. I went down on one knee, kissed her hand, and asked her to marry me.

"Maybe. Call me in one week. I must try to think before I say yes."

"Joe could marry us," I said. "There in the big chapel. Milly and you and Joe. My best friends."

"And the choir would sing 'Alleluia!'"

"Yes." We laughed together.

They left the next day. I was so full of hope. So full of love.

And she said yes. But by then the world was coming apart. I couldn't get there.

Earthquakes have wrecked the roads and bridges. The air is full of volcanic ash and cinders. Planes are crashing. Planes that fly are getting shot down with rockets. Someone is torpedoing ships at sea, especially those carrying people.

So, there she sits—alone. Here I sit—alone. She is full of regrets. "I should have…"

What does she mean, 'get her in trouble?' She must be too old to have children. But then she is always teasing.

Broke

"Now what do we do?" said Joe.

"Which problem?" Milly said.

"The missions in Africa and South America," he said. "They call, they write, they plead, food...medicine. People are starving, dying."

"You have spent and overspent," Milly said. "The Vatican is broke."

"But we must help."

"How?" she said. "You...Mr. Businessman. You know the limits."

"Then we borrow. Ask the World Bank for a half billion. We should have good credit."

"You're breaking your own rule," Milly said. "Never get too deep in debt."

"Can you call the U.S. Ambassador?" said Joe. "Ask for money? See if they can send help?"

"Their ships and planes are getting bombed," she said. "They can't get through."

"The missions say they can get supplies trucked in if they have money," Joe said. "Can you get them money?"

"Secret carriers," Milly said. "Money vouchers to the suppliers if we know them."

"Do it."

"I'm not trained in all this secret business," Milly said.

"Get help," he said. "Somebody here must know how. We must help!"

"Isn't this like a man that steals to help his neighbor knowing he can go to confession and be forgiven?"

"Ya," Joe said. "Christ will forgive us when he comes."
"I agree and disagree," she said.
"I know. But I must do anything to help."

Joe and Milly in Their Bedroom Embracing

"Oh, what's this?" Joe said. "Our glass ring around your neck?"

"I didn't want to forget it," she said. "In our rush out of here."

"Then you're back on my side again?"

"Did I leave you?" she said. "I took a vacation, but I couldn't forget you for a minute. It was a constant waiting...waiting to hurry back."

"I know—me too."

"Why don't we feel that way about God?" she said.

"She is with us all the time," said Joe.

"Yeah, but Christ said, 'I will be with you until the end of time.' Yet he leaves us, goes to heaven, and says, 'Here's the Holy Spirit.' Something is missing there."

"I keep thinking and thinking about this three in the God problem," Joe said. "Maybe only Christ is God. Someday he pretends to be the Father. Some days he puts on a dress and pretends to be the Holy Spirit."

"But the Holy Spirit that visited us was a woman, as much as I am a woman," Milly said.

"Yes, I know," Joe said. "But I've met very effeminate men."

"You're being silly. Don't tell the world that theory."

"I know I have to watch everything I say."

"Yeah."

"Sometimes I think that I understand, but it just disappears," Joe said. "Maybe I just understand words, not the real concept. Christ said that the rules of science and logic here on earth do not apply in heaven."

"You're rewording Christ again," Milly said. "I don't understand any of it either."

"I know."

"But you're thinking too much again," she said. "You need to get out to work. Go fix something."

"Yeah. I'm going to go get some super plaster repair. I'm going to fix that crumbling wall that bothers me so much."

"But that's what you have workers for. Tell them to do it."

"I can't," he said. "They're praying."

"Praying! Order them."

"I can see the newspaper get that. 'Pope orders workman to stop praying. And the world is ending!'"

"Yeah. Then forget it. It won't be here long."

"But the army taught me to keep improving our situation," Joe said.

"So do it," she said. "Maybe they'll help you later."

"Yeah, lead by example, not ordering…By the way. What about Lisa? Mike called. He's worried. I said we'd take care of her."

"All ships have a U.S. Navy escort now, but American citizens have first priority. Maybe later. I'll try my pull with the U.S. ambassador. I don't know why the Americans want to go home. It is worse there than here."

"I know. Mike said it is no fun living in Arizona anymore. He must stay. People will need his soup kitchens soon."

"And the people far away from him?" she asked.

"They starve; they will die. What can I do? I have no way to help so many. We need Christ's bread and fish miracle. I'm preparing another radio message for them, for the world. 'Read the words of Christ, pray for his love, and deliverance. Remember the Christian martyr's and their great pain, their great love. They are in heaven.'"

News

"A point of bad news you should know about," Milly said.

"Bad?" Joe said.

"You talked about people having fewer babies, so you have your fingers in the pie."

"Now what?"

"Doctors all over the world reported a drop in new pregnancies," she said. "Like one in ten."

"A 90 percent drop. Why?"

"They're blaming that terrible flu virus we had last winter," she said.

"I actually wanted to die."

"Me too," said Milly. "Anyway, it seems to have done more than killed millions of people."

"Very few old people left in the world," he said. "Killed the weak and feeble. Prophecy."

"Ya also now millions of people with defective sperm and eggs," she said. "Maybe even 10 percent of the pregnancies could still abort, maybe defective babies. They don't know yet."

"Prophecy. 'Gird the world for war.' That means get rid of the old and young."

"Ya no new grandchildren, no great grandchildren."

"I suppose my sperm are defective," Joe said.

"Don't worry," said Milly. "They won't ask you for a sample."

"No but think of the moral problems the doctors will have. They must save the human race.

"And the War?"

"I know," he said. "They're speeding toward disaster."

"Ya."

"Wait...a Bible connection."

"What?"

"The people most affected by the virus... the richer nations, the richer people," Joe said.

"So?"

"If the rich are sterile, Christ's words will come to pass sooner than we think."

"How's that?"

"The poor will inherit the world," Joe said.

"Ya. But after the great war, what a mess they will have."

"Ya—start over," said Joe.

The Call to Arms

"You received a nice letter from your son," Milly said. "He sent this other letter also."

"Other letter?" Joe said.

"From the U.S. Army. They want you to take a physical. See if you can do office duty."

"Me? They must be desperate."

"Must be, old men like you in the army."

"The Civil War had old men like me fighting," Joe said.

"The South was desperate."

"Ya the South," he said. "That reminds me, two of my classmates in officer training school. North Carolina."

"And?"

"They could not believe me; a Catholic would become an officer and fight for our country."

"What?" Milly said.

"Ya. Some religious nonsense. They felt the same way about a Jew."

"I can't believe it."

"I wonder if the Jewish guy ever made it—so immature, mama's boy, but determined," he said. "He was recycled. So, I never knew. Many, many friends I never knew what happened."

"I'll give this letter to the U.S. Ambassador to take care of."

"Ya."

"We had a long discussion last week, world situation," she said.

"And?"

"A great shortage of young men for the army, both U.S. and Europe," she said.

"Many?"

"Many...I mean fifty million men so they can have twenty-five million more for the military."

"You told him what I said?" Joe asked.

"Yes, God lets us suffer from our own sins," she said. "If we had stopped abortion over the last forty years, they would have the fifty million men."

"He agreed?"

"He had no answer."

"We did our share—nine children and twenty-five grandchildren."

"How many will fight? How many will die?"

"Sad...I still feel the deep-down feeling, the call to arms," he said.

"Your job is more important."

"I know."

A Few Rare Moments Alone Together in the Garden

"That song keeps coming back to me," Joe said. "'Kansas City.' Remember... we used to sing it and dance to it?"

"Yeah, we were so young," Milly said.

"When I first moved south, I met one of those crazy little women from there. She was crazier than you."

"You liked her?"

"Yeah. I mean I could have. She was engaged to someone back there. She left after a month. I could not stand isolation and mud roads."

"Back to Kansas City—bad move."

"What do you mean?"

"Earthquake, earth movement," she said. "Most of the city is under water and ice."

"Pray for them."

"Everyone, the west coast has millions of bodies," she said. "The ocean is running with them."

"They couldn't escape the tsunami?"

"Earthquakes wrecked the roads and bridges," she said. "There was no escape. A half million died in their cars! Wild disease outbreaks killing more."

"And atomic bombs?"

"Several, San Francisco had four."

"Yeah, Muslims hate homosexuals."

"It seems so," she said, "That city in southern France got three bombs too."

"And many more?"

"I am drawing up a map. But news is spotty."

"And Mike?"

"He gets through once in a while, mostly to Lisa. Priority communication for the pope."

"Yeah, and…?"

"So cold there he is ready to die. If he had any gas, he'd drive over to the volcanoes to warm up."

"Our children?"

"Surviving."

Letter from the Betrayer to Pope Joseph

I would call you friend Joseph, but I have betrayed you and I ask forgiveness. To an Arab, it is a double betrayal, worse than raping and killing the wife of your host. I beg Allah for forgiveness, yet he will still punish me, for I did it knowingly.

While I am evil, I must tell you that the leaders, the generals behind me, are as evil as the devil himself. Their plans to massacre all Christians are from the words of the devil. I am now only a figurehead. They are the power of the world retribution. They seek revenge. It is not domination they seek. It is death to all Christians, all over the world.

I speak up for you, for your safety. They laugh. They say all Christians are two-faced liars. They may pray to God but do the opposite of God's will, God's commandments.

I seek your safety, telling them you are a truly holy man. They laugh. "Cut off the head of all Christians. They will no longer fight as one.

I beg your forgiveness in love of Allah.

Sincerely,
Mohamed

Alone Before the Evening Meal

"You've been crying?" Joe said.

"My daughter Betty called," Milly said.

"Trouble?"

"Her son Craig was killed."

"The one in the army?"

"The atomic bomb at the training camp," Milly said.

"Ya the one at the officer training school. I heard," he said.

"My grandson dead," she said. "The first one dead."

"When I visited the President, I told him. I told the generals. I told them what they taught me, spread out the men. Atomic bombs kill for miles."

"They didn't listen," Milly said.

"I'm the pope. Keep my mind on religion."

"Betty is heartbroken."

"Thousands of mothers crying," Joe said. "The army has to have big parades. Thousands of officer candidates at one parade, thousands of sergeant trainees at another parade. Millions of tons of food in the middle… all gone."

"Suicide mission?"

"Probably, no one knows."

"What do we do?"

"Pray for the survivors," he said. "Call Betty in the morning. Let me talk to her."

"OK…what will you say?"

"I don't know…America's best young men and women turned to dust. What a waste."

"It's going to be a bad war."

"The worst possible."

"More of our grandchildren dead."

"Maybe all," he said. "It's sad."

The End Times

The pope has called a Vatican City meeting of important officials that could make it, clerical or not. About 280 men and women meet in the dark room. A hundred candles provide light and heat. There is no electric power. It is a terrible winter.

"We are meeting today to record for history the events of the world as we see them, what we are as a church attempting to do and what we except will happen," Joseph said. "We may all ask questions. We may all give suggestions on what to do. We all know we are in the end times as told in the Bible. We do not know when Christ is coming.

"We have met the Antichrist, that smooth talker, that super salesman. He came here as a Muslim peace maker. He made so many false promises. We made so many plans together. They will be entered into our recording. They are, of course, all broken promises.

"He learned our secrets, our plans, our world church system, and a list of every church and school, whatever. He went to NATO and learned their secrets, their bases. He traveled about the world in the name of peace, but he was learning secrets, military plans, weaknesses. He is now the moral leader of the Muslim Army. Tens of millions of men and growing. He has vast amounts of any weapons for his use. War could break out at any time.

"Surprisingly, we are not their main target. Who can read their minds? They respect our position of righteousness.

"Before I go on, will Father Damian give a report on the Swiss government?"

"Your Excellency, the Swiss, as always, remain neutral in this conflict," said Father Damian. "Their troops are on alert; many thousands protect their churches. They have recalled all their citizens except diplomats. They told our Swiss guards that they must come home, or they are on their own. Some have gone home, but many have come back, even older men. They are well armed but what is a thousand against millions of Muslims? Your guard has sworn to die to defend the papacy."

"Thank you, Father,..." said Joseph. "You all can look at this map later. Small atomic bombs have gone off all over the world, even one here in Rome. Millions of people have been killed...with this volcanic dirt, our world is dark, and a terrible winter is upon us. Food in the southern hemisphere is not growing. Starvation is growing everywhere.

"The ring of fire and the tsunami have killed millions of people and has destroyed all Pacific civilization.

"Father George, tell us the Japanese situation."

"Your excellency, the situation with Japan is grim," said Father George. "There were vast earthquakes and then the great slide you predicted. Millions are dead. The emperor, their government, and most of their financial center were destroyed. They are under martial law. Hourly tremors have kept the rest of the islands ready for more slides...as you predicted. Our catholic people are living in greater fear.

"As you know, their military leader wrote you a letter, blaming you, the pope, declaring war on the Vatican if we do not remove the curse you made on his country. You, the pope, talked to God to destroy his country. You are to blame for the slide.

"You sent Cardinal Chamblou as a special ambassador. His head came back to us frozen...by Fed Ex, with another letter.

"This letter stated, if there is another slide killing people, war is declared. Commandos will kill Catholics in churches around the world. Every Catholic in Japan will be executed. Priests will be tortured in terrible ways. Nuns will be raped and tortured. The Vatican will be attacked.

"So that is where we now are, waiting for another slide."

"It's hard to say thank you to that report, Father George," Joseph said. "Father Michael, the situation with NATO?"

"Your excellency. NATO is poised for war," said Father Michael. "Every kind and sort of weapon is ready to kill the Muslim army. The United States has almost a million personnel in and around Israel. European countries have more. Warships, planes, submarines, everything is ready. Atomic missiles around the world are aimed. Though many may be frozen, many have been drowned.

"I have no idea what will set off the war. How could anyone survive?

"Russia is holding back and protecting their own land, saying they are neutral. Atomic bombs have blown up a few churches. They know the power of the Muslim population. Russians live in fear.

"They and all the other surrounding countries have had large dissentions to the Muslim army. Former American friends are the same way. Egypt uses much of its army to protect American airfields which are not a good situation, of course. That alliance probably won't hold up.

"For the record, the first move was by the Muslim army. They moved troops across Turkey into the former Yugoslavia. They slaughtered every non Muslim. They got their revenge. Turkey was rocked with earthquakes. They could not defend themselves. They are not on good terms with NATO. Italy is much the same way. This church needs vast repairs."

"The destruction has only begun," Joseph said. "Major Lameau has his hand up."

"Your Excellency, you know our dedication to you and the office of the pope, but I, Major Lameau, am confused. I need advice."

"We are training for commando attack and Japanese fighting methods. But...how can we fight with all these people, thousands standing around? Are we to fire our machine guns with women and children right there?

What if they bring bombs, even an atomic bomb? What do we do? Can't these people go home?"

"I see the problem," Joseph said. "Anyone here with an idea, please write Major Lameau."

"But people are the church, the building is theirs. They are here to talk to God. Who are we to turn them away?"

"My wife will give a report on the United States," Joseph said.

"Shortly put," Milly said, "the United States is a giant, shaking, burning, dark icebox. Add to that the great damage done by the tsunami to both North and South America. Guam and Hawaii were almost washed clean. There is one deep wide split up the Mississippi River way up into Canada. There is another wide split up the Colorado River, but with branches like a saguaro cactus nine hundred miles long. Volcanoes are blowing up in several places. There is constant shaking from earthquakes, and lava is breaking out and running for miles in a hundred places. Forests and buildings are burning everywhere. The sky is black. Everywhere that is not burning is having the worst winter in history, times two. Great floods will occur if it ever does warm up.

"So, like everywhere else, people are dying by the millions from every cause. Eighteen atomic bombs have exploded in cities. Joe says more massive land movements are yet to come. Oh, God, help them."

"And our family?" Joseph said.

"Who knows. There is no communication, no power, no food, nothing."

"And the military?" Joseph said.

"They are trying to train vast numbers of men in the far south, like Arizona, even Mexico. But with difficulty; disaster is everywhere; food is short; fuel is short. Roads and bridges are gone. Airports are frozen and split. Train tracks are twisted. National guards are needed at home."

"But people survive?" Joseph said.

"Yes, from all reports," Milly said.

"And South America?"

"One small war, two threatening conflicts. Locusts, ants, animals going crazy," Milly said. "Massive earthquakes, volcanoes, atomic bombs, everything."

"And disease?"

"It is rampart all around the world," Milly said. "The medical business has no electric power, no heat, little medicine; the world's military has taken most of the medicine. It is too cold to make more. Gas pipes are broken everywhere."

"And Africa?" Joseph asked.

"There were two uprisings, three threatening wars, and everything else—bugs, earthquakes. Across North Africa are millions of men, Muslim men, walking or driving toward Mecca. They are ready to die for Allah," Milly said.

"All around the world, even the U.S., Muslim pilots are stealing planes, even bombers, commercial jets, fighters. They are joining the Muslim Army."

"Australia?" Joseph asked.

"Very cold summer and extra dry, threats of invasion—especially bug invasion.

"There is an enormous NATO fleet there preparing for war."

"Southeast Asia?"

"China is invading Southward," Milly said. "They too are cold beyond belief; their food is gone.

"Northern Chinese and Mongolians are moving in mass toward the Muslim Army. They eat the very dirt. They are now getting provisions air-dropped along the way."

"And India?"

"Over fifteen atomic bombs, maybe a billion dead in the region," Milly said. "The Muslim army has taken over. There is mass slaughter of non Muslims. They have spared Catholics so far."

"And the Muslim Army?"

"They say, 'As many men as there are grains of sand around Mecca.' They are highly trained. Generals have war college training under NATO or the U S. schools. They have atomic weapons and rockets of all sorts. Thousands of planes of all sorts, many U.S. trained pilots.

"The U.S. military is separating Muslims, putting them on noncrucial duty...like mass burials on the west coast.

"Hundreds of thousands of Muslim men are joining the Muslim army every week. Ship loads, everything, everywhere, even Indonesia.

"And nobody to stop this great Muslim army ... except NATO?" Joseph asked. "They are vastly outnumbered."

"No human army could stop them," Milly said.

"That is the real answer. No human..." Joseph said.

Last Letter from Mike

To my friends,

    Enclosed is a separate letter to Lisa.

    There is no longer phone service, so I hope you get this letter.

    Life is dark and dreary. But the people I serve are stoic. We have our happy get-togethers.

    I do your request, feed the people. A few thousand Native Americans will survive because of your foresight. I drive your electric car to fourteen factories each week. I eat fourteen meals per week; the people are lucky to get this one good meal. Sometimes I find a priest to travel with me to say Mass for our crowd. We have electric lights because of your foresight. Your friends at Southwest Wind Power provided us well—reliable wind generators. Solar cells are useless as we seldom see the sun. Light, water pumps everything. The priest and I thank you for our daily shower. I feel guilty. We even hear the radio news.

    The army has asked us to begin production of various items, so we are retooling and getting ready. They have taken all our young men and women. It is like they disappear. There is no communication.

    Earthquakes are frequent. Roads and bridges are broken, so I have a tough time traveling. I carry a shovel and extra jacks.

    I would much rather be with you all. Hope you get this world mess settled, but I remember what you said.

    All my love,
    Mike

The Beginning of the End

"Well, it's happened," Joe said. "The U.S. has its proof. Now they must retaliate. The war has begun."

"What happened?" Milly asked.

"The Muslim Army set off the atomic bombs in the air at Tucson, Phoenix, and Yuma, then training centers all around the same areas. They killed hundreds of thousands of trainees. One bomb did not go off. They caught the suicide-bomber. He led them to the base out in the desert. The Mexican army led the fire fight. In the rush, that bomb did not go off either. So, there was proof. All the base personnel had put on their Muslim army uniforms, a ton of paperwork proved everything."

"We're leaving Rome now?" Milly asked.

"No, we will wait until the Holy Spirit tells us. The Swiss guard has everything ready."

"And the annulment applications?"

"Let them burn," Joe said. "If the people survive, let them ask Christ."

"Shouldn't I go clean and vacuum our new home?"

"It's being done," Joe said. "We take a squad of Swiss guard. The rest will head home. When we get the Holy Spirit's say, we jump in a Jeep and head for the mountains. We will have all symbols of authority with us. Many holy religious items are already there. When we get to the city limits, we call the Rome commandant and tell him to evacuate the city. We have discussed the situation."

"Do you think the Holy Spirit will forget us?" she asked.

"When you were working, did you forget your sick child?" he asked.

"...then I will be with you. Will I see Christ?"

"I don't know," Joe said. "But I am only half a man, half a pope without you."

"Some math that is. You and me, one and one makes three, but without me you are only half."

"Yeah. Love makes strange math."

"So, we'll hide in a cave?"

"No, we will broadcast to the world. The pope is alive and well. The pope is the symbol of love, hope, and peace. But Christ will have to take care of the peace."

My Letter

I found a copy of this letter that I sent to Joe about six months after they left. I copied the letter so I could remember what I had said. Joe never answered my questions, even though we talked about the business once or twice a week. I supposed he was too busy for me.

> Dear Joe:
>
> I need to talk, but you are a busy man. Pope of the world and phone time to Europe is not cheap. Your words, "Money better spent helping the poor."
>
> So let me vent my feelings.
>
> You are telling the world that you had a visitor, a woman who called Herself God. I know you two cannot lie. Yet I cannot believe you. After all I've had a few honeymoon hallucinations of my own, not quite so spectacular...
>
> All these years of Santa Claus, Rudolph, Easter Bunny and on and on make me quite skeptical. Isn't God just another make-believe person? How can I believe what I cannot see?
>
> If there could be such thing as a devil, wouldn't he invent space aliens, bigfoot, the Loch Ness Monster? Create misbelief and mistrust? God is like one of them.
>
> We have both worked with *the People*. I saw your love and dedication. You saw mine. Where does this depth of feeling come from? I must dedicate each moment of my life to helping them. There can be no vacation. There is no time for God. Where is He? She?

You said God helped you win money at Vegas. He gave you numbers for the state lottery, money for the business. Now you make me wonder. But isn't that cheating? God helped you cheat? But you did bring in a few million dollars.

The other day I heard that old saying, "I think, therefore I am." So, I thought. How do I know that I think? What is inside me?

You have mentioned your past life, and I feel I have had more than one also. I wish I could see a hypnotist. But what is inside me that had that past life?

You two have left me alone to run this company. Even the three of us hardly kept up. I know we talk. You help with so many problems. I feel your support, but I am lonely.

If there is a Holy Spirit, does She feel the same way I do? Being left alone to take care of this world? Maybe that's why all the work is not getting done (e.g., accidents, etc.)? I cannot do it all either. I miss you both, in so many ways. Remembering the good times doesn't get the work done.

And no winning lottery numbers! Never enough money to pay all the bills. I need help, both of you. But I know you have your problems too.

You said to go to church, so I drop into a mission when I can. It helps my loneliness. Sometimes they read your "Letter to My Friends of Christ." It makes me so proud. I want to yell out, "That's my friend Joe." But I keep quiet and just shake everyone's hands with gusto.

Later I want to go outside and shout "There is no God. The church is deceiving everyone."

But I don't. I can offend you or distract from your teaching. I know these people need moral fiber and a reason for living, whatever church they attend.

I don't need it. I have only one reason for living, to help *the People*. I don't break anybody's law, man's or God's. I eat right, drink little, drive carefully.

But God is impossible.

But you are real, my friend on and off for over forty-five years. It is utterly impossible for you to be the pope. But you are.

So many other things about us are impossible, but they are.

So, I have no answer.

I see life. I see the human body as impossible to chance.

So, when I come to see you and Milly, you'll show me the impossible God pointing to the impossible Adam and Eve, and maybe I'll get inspired. Too many impossibilities might lead to an answer.

Impossible in my own way.

Love to you both,
Mike

At a later date, I found the source of all love.
Quietly...peacefully.